Wounded Healers

True Life Stories of 12 Courageous Women touched by the Healing of Jesus Christ

By
Wounded Healers' Authors

Sue Alexander
Alison Beale
Jean-Ann Cooper
Courtney Diehl
Michele Dudas
Denise Gardner
Jade Getchell
Susan Hamilton
Sue Leonard
Therese Shelesky
Tammy Stewart
Amanda Summers

Copyright 2017.

The book authors retain sole copyright to
their contributions to this book.

Published 2017.

Printed in the United States of America.

All rights reserved.

No portion of this book may be reproduced, stored in a retrieval system, or transmitted in any form or by any means – electronic, mechanical, photocopy, recording, scanning, or other – except for brief quotations in critical reviews or articles, without the prior written permission of the author.

ISBN 978-1-943650-46-0

Bilbe references from
NEW INTERNATIONAL VERSION
ENGLISH STANDARD VERSION
KING JAMES BIBLE
NEW AMERICAN STANDARD BIBLE
NEW LIVING TRANSLATION
BEREAN STUDY BIBLE

This book may be ordered from
www.bookcrafters.net and other online bookstores.

Published by BookCrafters, Parker, Colorado.
www.bookcrafters.net

Dedication

*This book is dedicated to our Lord Jesus Christ
and those He blessed us with to bring the book to fruition.
May the stories bring Him glory and bless women in
need of hope, encouragement and healing.*

Acknowledgements

Cara Buzzell, Creative Design
Wounded Healers book and Women of THE WAY Ministries website

Stephen G. Shelesky, Financial Support
Women of THE WAY Ministries

Sue Leonard, Content Editing and Independent Publishing Guidance
Wounded Healers book

Stephen G. Shelesky, II, Website Administration
Women of THE WAY Ministries website

Angel Sponsors
(You know who you are...thank you for your support!)

Joe and Jan McDaniel, Editing, Interior Design, and Publishing
Wounded Healers (thank you for your patience!)

INTRODUCTION

I remember sitting by the fireplace in my front room praying for each of the writers whose personal blogs linked to a website the Lord moved me create in 2013. Daily devotionals, weekly Psalms, discipleship writings, and various life stories offered from each of the writers populated the Women of the Way Ministries site. As I read the life stories over the first year, I felt a tug from the Holy Spirit, but it wasn't clear what I was being led to do. Then, during a quiet time, there was a stirring in my heart. God clearly spoke about the need for this book, a book where each writer would not only share their testimony with you, but also share their trials and triumphs. Moreover, in spite of seemingly insurmountable challenges, share how God had changed their lives for the better.

It took some time to gather the twelve writers featured here. Several were bloggers from the Women of The Way Ministries portal website, others were friends of the bloggers and a few were women who crossed my path at some point in time. Though many were eager to share their story; others were initially unsure of disclosing the details of their lives to the world. Some were downright frightened that family and friends might come to know a dark side of their past that had been a secret. However, with lots of prayers, and by the grace of God, they stepped up and said, "Yes!" I readily commend each and every one for their courage!

The stories you will read include tremendous heartbreak and loss. Challenges that, without the power of the Lord, would have been insurmountable. Each and every one of these women pinpoints the moment that God showed up in their lives. Moreover, the timing in each case was, of course, perfect.

As you move from story to story, you will recognize challenges that are similar to your own, or to one of your family members or friends. Stories of deceit, betrayal, mental illness, eating disorders, and the loss of relationships and loved ones. In some cases, the challenge remains, but these women had the courage to transform from victim to victor in Christ, Jesus.

I hope you find that "Wounded Healers" is an appropriate title for this book. You will come to know that the wounds are deep, and the scars are still there. However, the scars are part of each woman's identity and prove they survived and are thriving in the Lord's love, grace and forgiveness.

These wounded women have poured out their hearts in hopes that someone like you, might do as they did and seek the Lord Jesus Christ for hope, encouragement and healing.

My prayers go with you, my friend.

Therese Shelesky

A personal thanks to my friend and *Wounded Healers* writer, Jean-Ann Cooper, for helping me capture just the right words for the Introduction of *Wounded Healers*.

TABLE OF CONTENTS

The Awakening
    Sue Alexander...1
Go and Love
    Alison Beale..9
A Case of Mistaken Identity
    Jean-Ann Cooper..23
Just Like Me
    Courtney Diehl..36
It's Never Too Late
    Michele Dudas...42
Trials Blessed by One Another
    Denise Gardner...50
Greater the Victory the Greater the Battle
    Jade Getchell...58
Dangerous Times and Oblivious Parenting
    Susan Hamilton..70
Faith From My Own Perspective
    Sue Leonard..80
Too Many Mistakes
    Therese Shelesky..84
The Darkest Journey
    Tammy Stewart..96
When Only God Can Heal
    Amanda Summers...117

The Awakening

Sue Alexander

My eyes were struggling to adjust to the bright lights that glared overhead. Slowly the room came into focus. It looked like a hospital recovery room, and my husband peered over me intently, his expression serious. Alarm bells went off! Where was I? How did I get there? *What happened to me?*

I learned that I had been in a psychiatric hospital for six weeks undergoing electro-convulsive therapy, formerly known as "shock" treatments. Before they began I had completely lost touch with reality, and that morning in the recovery room when I "awakened" was the first time I had been fully conscious in weeks. I was an active wife and mother, one of the pastors of a successful and growing church, and a vital member of the community. I looked at my husband in shock. *How did this happen?*

This was 2011 and the 2008 recession had hit our mountain ski town very hard. Many people were experiencing severe financial crises, and when I preached earlier that year I had said, "I did not know that so many people I care about could all be hurting at the *same* time." I now realize I was struggling and overwhelmed, too. In addition to working long hours in full-time ministry, I was also desperate to find nursing care for my aging mother in another state. Also, one of our daughters was in a life crisis, so there was plenty of stress in my life. But I had a long history of facing tough problems and overcoming them, including my husband's early alcoholism and a fractured marriage, my brother's untimely death, heartaches with kids and some financial reverses, but this time, challenges were coming at me from every direction and all at the same time. It was the perfect storm, and I was in the center.

The previous year I had experienced some heart problems which did not turn out to be serious, but were frightening enough that I had become hesitant to exercise outdoors alone and my world began to shrink. The cardiac issues also resulted in a doubled dose of the drug Xanax I had taken for heart palpitations for over thirty years, and it was a lot for my small size and weight.

Xanax can be addictive, mainly because it is so effective at reducing anxiety. Calming relief comes very quickly, but unfortunately dissipates rapidly leaving one waiting for the next dose. I did not dream this prescription drug, which had helped me for so many years, could be dangerous or might be part of the reason I ended up with a psychotic break.

Before I was hospitalized, my level of anxiety was so high that I could not sleep, barely ate, and I finally was so out of it that I required full time care. My husband had to take the pills away from me and dole them out. He frantically sought medical care and eventually took me to a Denver hospital.

It was a very distressing time for him and our daughters as they wondered if I would ever "come back." Together they made the difficult decision to approve the ECT treatments, and gratefully they worked!

After six weeks of treatment I was able to return home to begin to reconstruct my life with my husband's help. I felt like Lazarus! The first thing I had to do was embrace the story I was hearing second-hand, but everything felt so surreal. It's a good thing I trusted the story-tellers or I would not have believed the tales they told. For example, I left our daughter's home in Denver in the middle of the night after I was released from the hospital and went for a walk in the neighborhood, and I did not remember a thing! It was the dog that woke up my husband to alert him that I had left the house, and I am sure my family wondered if the hospital dismissal was warranted at that point!

Along with the facts came a flood of *shame*. I started the blame game, and I pointed at me. Shame is different from guilt where we feel

The Awakening

we *did* something wrong. Shame tells us there is something inherently wrong *with us*, and I believe as women we are often quick to take responsibility. It was very difficult to return to church, as it doesn't get more humbling than being in a psychiatric hospital. Instead of sitting in my usual place in the front, I slipped in the back, imagining what people might be thinking. It would have been easier to say I had cancer. People would have hugged me and told me they were sorry.

Sad to say, we are uncomfortable with mental illness and often don't have language for it.

I spent a lot of time that autumn recovering alone, but the one relationship I diligently pursued was with a therapist. Because this whole experience had been frightening for my husband, he became anxious if I seemed to have a "down" day, so I was reluctant to share my feelings. My therapist helped me recognize I could experience a negative emotion and not slide back into the abyss of anxiety and depression. She encouraged me to feel and acknowledge my emotions, as burying emotions is the least healthy thing we can do, because we bury them alive! I would share my concerns and she would respond, "Sue, that's a *normal* emotional response for this particular situation." Normal became my favorite word!

Three good friends had taken turns caring for me before I was hospitalized, and they seemed so astonished at how well I was doing, I finally begged one of them to tell me how *bad* it had really been. One reluctantly told me I had stated emphatically, "The devil has won, and I belong to him." I cringed when I heard I had denied the God I loved and served and Who had been so faithful to me over the years.

I went for a walk in tears that blustery fall day. But it wasn't long before God's gentle, quiet voice whispered in my heart, *I give them eternal life, and they shall never perish; no one will snatch them out of my hand.* (John 10:28) I was overwhelmed with the comfort and love that filled my aching heart. God had kept me. God had not let me go. *He* knew that my words were not my true heart's intention. I was sick. And He had taken care of me.

Suddenly I could see that the few fuzzy memories of the hospital were not the whole picture. God was there! The following weekend a phrase in a worship song caught my attention, "You danced over me when I was unaware." Tears flowed again. Not tears of sadness this time, but tears of joy! Waves of truth washed over me as the words I will never leave you or forsake you (Hebrews 13:5) came to life for me.

One thing was certain: I could *not* return to my old ways. I could not resume my unbalanced, too busy life. I realized that I could not *allow* anxiety and fear to dominate my mind. The Bible says, *Do not **let** your heart be troubled.* (John 14:1) I realized that I had choices and I learned to be very vigilant over my thought life. Upon reflection, I realized how often I had not *monitored* my thinking and was often unaware of what was going on in my mind. I believe this is true for most of us. Our minds are so often busy, thinking of the next meeting or errand, or constantly distracted with buds in our ears and our eyes on our phones.

Through Dr. Caroline Leaf's enlightening book entitled *Who Switched Off My Brain?* I learned that when we think negative thoughts over 30 toxic hormones are released into our bodies. There is even a specific "fear" hormone called ACTH. Over the years I had flooded my body with a toxic chemical bath that affected me down to the cellular level. In addition, *repeated* negative thoughts build very strong pathways in our brains and then our negative thoughts become *automatic*. No wonder the Bible says we are to *take our thoughts captive.* (2 Corinthians 10:5) This means we cannot allow them free rein. We have to lasso them and replace them with the truth and with scripture. We *can* change our thinking, and we can actually change our brains!

When we think positive thoughts, like gratitude, compassion, forgiveness and love we release good chemicals like serotonin and dopamine. It is our *choice* every day to choose the chemical environment of our bodies, and making these choices has been some of the hardest work I have ever done.

In addition to becoming aware of my thinking, I realized that for much of my life I had been propelled by my schedule, barely pausing to take a breath. A full, scribbled calendar meant I must be accomplishing something! Our culture has made busyness a virtue, and it can be accentuated in the Christian world because we believe we are busy

The Awakening

"for God." I realized, too, how much of my identity was wrapped up in "doing." Now I had to learn to "be," and to thoughtfully plan spaces in my life. If I started to feel anxious I had to deal with it *drug* free. Time with God, long walks, and deep breathing slowly replaced the little peach pills. The day finally came when feeling stressed felt foreign to me, whereas before it had been my norm. That's when I knew I was making progress!

It might not surprise you to learn that I went through a period where I was afraid I might go backwards. Simply driving my car the first time was terrifying, and later it took all the courage I could muster to drive to Denver and face the city traffic. If I felt afraid to do something, I had to face it and do it! Fear is a terrible taskmaster, and it took practice to wrestle back control. And if I couldn't remember something, I felt a twinge of fear. But then I would have lunch with someone my age and realize that it was probably normal!

God was also very gracious to give me reassurance. During my recovery, I taught a class called "The Voice," which was not about music but rather hearing God. One week I cut pictures out of magazines, laid them out in the room, played quiet music and asked the participants to ask God to speak to each of them through a photo. I was not planning to do it myself, but I ended up joining the group and one photo jumped out at me. It was a picture of two little Japanese girls in kimonos walking under an umbrella. It looked as if the rain had stopped, but the umbrella was still up. I heard God say, "You can put the umbrella away, Sue. The storm has passed." I have that picture framed in my office today, a constant reminder of God's promise to me.

As I prayed about what might have contributed to my illness, one thing God revealed was I had unwittingly started to trust my own competency. Years of effectively ministering to people had caused me to rely on myself rather than on God. Early in my life with Christ I learned that the Bible teaches *Without me (Jesus) you can do nothing.* (John 15:5) Consequently, I had consciously depended on Him through all sorts of trials and difficulties and as I ministered to others, and it was amazing to watch Him work.

This shift to self-reliance did not happen overnight. It happened subtly as I became good at what I did. God's word says, *If you think you are standing strong, be careful not to fall.* (I Corinthians 10:12)

But I was too busy to pay attention. There were many times when I would hurry out the door in the morning to meet someone and tell God I was glad He understood that I didn't have time to spend time with Him. But after the harrowing breakdown, dependence on God became my norm again.

When the one year anniversary of my hospitalization approached, I felt unsettled and made an appointment with my therapist. She was discerning and said, "Sue, you may not have conscious memories of this time, but your *body* does. We remember on a *cellular* level." She also said, "Grief, or remembering, is like a television set that turns on in the corner of your mind. You don't get to turn it on, and you don't get to turn it off. Sometimes you can distract yourself, and sometimes you need to pay attention." It was very good advice. She suggested I pay attention and write something to commemorate the anniversary, and I ended composing the following Psalm:

>Why pause to remember when memories often carry pain?
>Our deeper selves are calling to us silently,
>shouting all the same.
>
>Fearfully made, the Psalmist tells me
>so complex, so deep, unmined.
>A part of self that is mysterious,
>but present, nonetheless.
>
>God was there in shadows, watching,
>measuring every ounce of pain.
>*He drew the boundaries of my desolation*
>*And brought me back to me again.*
>
>He has taken what was broken,
>changed my life in many ways.
>Life was lived too often mindless,
>now I treasure all my days.

The Awakening

> How can I begin to praise Him,
> thank Him for my life restored?
> Living life with all my senses,
> Even better than before.
>
> Now my heart is here to serve Him,
> Now my mind can praise again.
> Wholeness...spirit, soul and body
> *Amplified to praise His name!*

Yes, God drew the boundaries of my desolation. I can honestly say that five years later, I am grateful for this dark experience. I share my story freely because so many people struggle with depression and anxiety and other mental health issues and believe the lie that they are unique and they are alone. Too many Christians are disheartened when told they should "just believe" or that depression/anxiety is sin. But the brain is an organ, like the liver or the heart, and things can go wrong.

Yes, our thinking can make us sick. But sometimes there are very real, organic issues in our brains. Because *electricity* helped my brain to work again, there was obviously a very real *physiological* element involved. It wasn't all in my "head." Neuroscience is exploding today, and we are just beginning to understand the complexities of the brain and what we call the "mind."

Prescription drugs for anxiety and depression are used by millions of people in our country, and I am not against drugs per se. Many have been helped by these drugs. But they can be misused. They can be over-prescribed. When too much is taken for too long, the effects can be serious like they were for me. I am simply saying be careful.

Your story may be different from mine, and in reality not everyone gets a happy ending. Some people have similar experiences but continue on to Alzheimer's or dementia. But for those of us who come out on the other side, the great challenge is to *live differently.*

Every day I ask God to bring people across my path who can be encouraged by my story, and I make sure they know the great part God played in it. I love Jesus' name *Emmanuel*, which is translated "God *with* us." One year I kept my undecorated, but lighted Christmas tree, in my living room well into January. It was a sweet reminder to me that Jesus wasn't put away with the Christmas boxes. He is *always* with us, and I will *never* forget the weeks He was Emmanuel, *with me*, in the loneliness of a spare room in a hospital in another city. And I will be forever grateful.

Sue Alexander

Go and Love

Alison Beale

I'm broken. Are you?

I believe we are all broken people because we are human. We love, we hurt, and we make mistakes. Brokenness is often recognized by its side effects on our lives— pain, anxiety, loss, anger, and jealousy, to name a few. The most dangerous kind of brokenness, though, is the kind we don't recognize. The kind defined by entitlement, lack of gratitude, and the selfishness of living only within the confines of our own lives. It can manifest itself in complacency, a lack of compassion, or an inability to feel true happiness, because what we have is never deeply satisfying. It's easy to always want more in our culture, because there is so much out there for us to want—newer, better, or more extravagant things than we already have. Don't get me wrong; it's not "wanting more" that's the issue. It's healthy and productive to have goals to work toward and it's natural to want things. The problem comes when we feel entitled to things and everything becomes about us, because entitlement is an unhealthy perspective and I believe that selfishness leads to an empty heart.

Let's talk about my life for a minute. My parents are divorced, and I grew up in an environment of unending, stressful family drama. I graduated from Belmont University. It's a good school, but it's definitely not Harvard. I live in a one-bedroom apartment and drive a Honda Civic with a dent in the side. I can't afford to shop at Whole Foods, even though I'd like to. I only buy clothes off the clearance rack. Maybe one day I'll have enough money to get venti drinks at Starbucks whenever I feel like it.

Well, does that sound spoiled or what? Yes, the perspective is one of entitlement. If I thought like that, I'd never be happy because I'd never be truly satisfied. I have acted both selfishly and unselfishly throughout my life. I have found that when I act selfishly and feel entitled, things don't go my way. I become grumpy, disappointed, and even more hyper-focused on my "negative" situation. There were many times when I threw fits, acted ungrateful, or acted like some tiny problem was the end of the world. While this still happens on occasion, I now realize that my attitude of entitlement caused me to live with blinders on and from the wrong perspective. When I was so caught up in my own world, I was unable to see the beauty of the world around me. That's not something I want to miss out on, because there is so much to appreciate!

Now, let's look at my life from an enlightened perspective. I am privileged. My life, like anyone else's, hasn't been without its challenges. But I have always lived a very comfortable life, having a loving and supportive family, a college education, no student loans, a home, a reliable car, a job in a field I love, pets, spending money, clean water and a fridge full of nutritious food. This week, my biggest struggle was when my dryer stopped working and I had to set foot in the laundromat. At first I was annoyed, but I forced myself to remember that I am not entitled to a dryer. It is a privilege. Just like I am not entitled to my loving and supportive family, who is always there for me. Not everyone has that, so I am very blessed. My college education? I was unbelievably privileged to attend college without having to worry about paying my own tuition. While college is the norm for many people in America, it is not even an option for some. My job, my car, my home, access to healthy food and water? I am not entitled to any of it. But I have the good fortune to be able to drink a ton of water every day, take hot showers and have a toilet. I am lucky, and I am one of the few with these privileges.

Our perspectives, outlooks, goals, and passions are all influenced by people and experiences that shape who we become. Personally, I have been shaped (and by shaped I mean flipped, crushed, moved, and put back together in a new way) by global missions. Classic— privileged American white girl visits third world country to help and has a life-changing experience. Cliché? Maybe. But how do things become clichés in the first place? Repetition, widespread experience, truth.

I have traveled to Port-au-Prince, Haiti and Kijabe, Kenya on mission trips where I learned what true happiness is. I've learned it from people who have nothing, materially speaking. That irony is not lost on me.

✳✳✳

I stepped out of the Port-au-Prince airport, looked around, and felt like I had been punched in the stomach when I observed the run-down area around me and looked over at the group of people hanging around the airport. It somewhat resembled a run down, deserted festival—tattered tents, dirt ground, broken fences. I was met with desolate stares. Although my mission team surrounded me, I definitely felt out of place. We got on the bus and began our drive to the hotel. Our guide told us that the rubble on the street was from the earthquake that had occurred three years prior. I looked out the window and saw endless tents—"tent cities," as they are called. Most of the people living in these tents were still displaced from the earthquake. The environment was very stimulating, but I was experiencing some culture shock. That first bus ride was the scariest drive of my life; I had to close my eyes a few times as we frequently were inches away from hitting goats, cows, children, and motorcycles. To add to the culture shock, we were told that it is seen as an insult to the driver if you wear your seatbelt.

Our hotel was the nicest in the city. In America, it'd be considered a crappy motel. But it was charming, and I was just happy I didn't see any giant spiders. The first night, I had a hard time falling asleep, mostly because of the sound of fighting dogs that filled the city. It was vicious, and the worst was when I heard the whimpers and yelps of dying dogs. I remember lying awake thinking that I wasn't sure I could handle it, and I seriously doubted my decision to come to Haiti. Now, those doubts sound ridiculous. Oh, I didn't think I could handle witnessing the poverty and distress that is reality for millions of people? Luckily,

I quickly realized that being out of my comfort zone was a good thing. There's a lot to learn in this world, and living in ignorance is no way to go through life. My first big realization was that no substantial personal growth happens when you're comfortable. I then knew I needed to "get comfortable" with being uncomfortable.

✳✳✳

Going to Haiti, I thought I'd be entering a country of grief-stricken, unhappy people. I have never been more wrong. The people and children I observed, spoke to, and played with were the epitome of beauty. Their joy was contagious and their genuine gratitude was inspiring. Our team was building a house for a wonderful woman named Kazi and her family. Kazi's son-in-law, Wilson, helped us build the house. To this day, thinking about Wilson makes me smile. He has no idea how much he changed my life. I even named my cat Wilson, after him. Weird? Yeah, but I love this guy. Wilson was quiet for most of the week we were in Haiti. We all assumed he didn't speak English. On one of our last days, a few of us sat in the house with Wilson during our lunch break, sharing crackers and protein bars with him. We noticed on our first day that the Haitian workers didn't stop to eat lunch, so we essentially forced them to accept some of our food and take a break every day. Wilson was wearing jeans and a polo shirt, one of his few outfits, and had on shoes with holes in them. My immediate thought was that shoes with holes aren't safe for a construction site, but the sad realization set in that he didn't have a choice. He was thin — too thin. Seeing this incredible person, while processing the fact that his slight form was due to malnourishment, hurt my heart. It hurts even now to think about. Of course I was aware that malnourishment is a serious problem, but I understood it on a whole new level when it looked me in the eyes.

As we ate, we started talking with Wilson and found that he actually spoke very good English. His voice was quiet and gentle, but he spoke with great passion. He was in his late twenties and going to school to become an engineer. His wife Stephanie had recently given birth to a baby boy. Wilson spoke of his marriage to Stephanie with joy and told us how important it was to him, despite marriage being something that is not commonly valued in Haiti. He told us about Kazi's love for Jesus, saying, "She wakes up every day so happy and thankful for what God has blessed her with."

This is a woman who has next to nothing, and it was so beautiful to hear about the joy that God brings her. Wilson shared his love for God with our group as well, saying, "I'm constantly praying... in the morning, when I am working, when I am eating, and at night. I am so grateful for what God has blessed me with and that I have the opportunity to work and go to school."

Before I went to Haiti, I didn't realize what a privilege it was to be able to work and go to school. Work and school were normal, expected, and routine for me. Hearing Wilson say how grateful he was to be able to work (as in physical labor building houses in intense heat!) was a much-needed reality check for me. Before singing and dancing for us, which were Wilson's favorite activities, he shared one more beautiful lesson.

"Christians, no matter where they live or what they do, are all united and part of an embassy of God."

***

Alison Beale

I traveled to Kijabe, Kenya in May of 2014 with the wonderful organization Love Africa. Love Africa has been active in Kijabe for several years, so they have great connections in the area. My group and I were able to do some valuable work as a result. One man they partner with is John Njane (pronounced John Johnny, which is fun to say). John Njane has dedicated his life to helping his fellow Kenyans and fully embodies Psalm 68:5, *A father to the fatherless, a defender of widows, is God in His holy dwelling.* He has taken in a dozen orphaned boys off the street, started programs that teach women to sew and farm, runs a local shop, helps build houses for those in need, delivers food to several widows every month, and just helps anyone and everyone in any way he can. This guy is the closest thing to Superman the world has.

Part of our group spent one morning delivering food to widows with John. We brought sacks of food to their homes to make sure they at least had enough food to feed themselves and their families for a few weeks. Although the women were elderly widows, most of them cared for grandchildren or orphans they had taken in. Since they aren't physically able to make the journey to get food and carry it home, they rely on John Njane to help feed their families. These women were so wonderful, loving on us as if we were their own children. African hospitality is profound. They each wanted a picture with our group because John prints out the photos and brings them back to the women. Such excitement over taking a photo with us! They were so grateful to John and to our group for bringing them food, spending time with them, and giving them photos to remember us by.

One thing that struck me right away in Kenya, just as it had in Haiti, is how much people value spending time with each other. In the United States, we rush around, make plans, and focus on how busy we are, hardly making time for others like we should. Spending time with people we love should be our priority, not something we pencil in to fit our schedule.

When we arrived in Kenya we were told about "African time." Essentially, everyone is always late and events or meetings rarely start on time. Interaction with people and building relationships is their priority. Having a great conversation or spending time with someone they care about takes priority over anything else. It was refreshing to experience such a loving, people-centered environment instead of the task-centered environment I'm used to in the United States. As we visited the widows, it was so clear how special we made each of their days just by stopping by and showing we care about them. I also realized it went both ways. It was special to us, too, because of how special it was for them. It really is that simple.

John took us to the home of the poorest family in the village, a woman who takes care of fourteen orphans. Until recently, there had been fifteen orphans, but one of them passed away. When we arrived at the home, she wasn't there. But three young children were, perhaps aged twelve, eight and two. The oldest was mentally disabled, and each child was covered in dirt: dirty clothes, dirty feet, dirty faces. The oldest child was only wearing a long shirt. The middle child comforted the crying toddler. The worn look in his eyes resembled that of someone much older than eight. My heart broke as I saw them alone, while their caretaker was most likely off doing what work she could. John told us that being home alone meant the woman could not afford to send them to school for that term. "What is the cost of school?" a person in our group asked. John said, "For a three-month term it costs about $4 per child." In that moment I experienced a sinking feeling, the kind where it physically feels like your heart and stomach drop. I was devastated and ashamed. All it takes is $4 to send a child to school. I thought

about how quickly I spend $4 and how little value that amount of money has to me. In Kenya, $4 means an education, which is the only thing that gives those children a fighting chance at a bright future.

We walked into their home, which was a hut about half the size of my one-bedroom apartment. Fifteen people had to live and sleep there, and to put it in perspective, only about three of us walked through the hut at a time because otherwise it was too crowded. There was one old bed frame with springs, and John said that it was a luxury for

whichever child got to sleep on it. The rest slept on the dirt floor. There were no pillows, and maybe three tattered blankets. I don't think there was a dry eye in our group. Realizing those living conditions were reality day in and day out for so many people was stifling, heartbreaking, and overwhelming. I felt helpless. I could help them somewhat in that moment, but what about all of the others? The millions of people living in those conditions? The millions dying from starvation, contaminated water, or lack of basic medical care? Who would help them? We need more people like John Njane. Let's be those people.

Since my visit to Kenya, I have learned that John successfully arranged for a couple of mattresses to be given to that family. Does that solve all of their problems? Of course not, but I was elated to learn that their quality of life was lifted even just a little bit.

***

On my fourth day in Kenya, part of our mission team visited Kijabe Hospital. People from all over the country come to this hospital because it is the best available. Traveling to it is a huge commitment and is no easy feat. The hospital was decent, but would be nowhere close to acceptable in the U.S. I was grateful that the staff is able to care for so many people, but sad that this is the absolute best care available and people sacrifice so much to travel there.

The children's ward was heartbreaking. We talked to patients and mothers with sick babies. Most of the people were happy to see us and didn't mind talking to us. I was impressed with their openness. If I were in a hospital, especially with a sick child, I would not want strangers conversing with me. Even in the worst situations, Kenyan people are friendly and kind.

At the hospital I was with Kim and Karla, two of the girls on my team. We met Mary, who was staying in one of the rooms with her eight-month-old son Gavin. We sat down next to her and said, "Hello," not knowing that her story would shatter us.

A few months earlier, while she was washing clothes in the river, Mary's three-year-old son and baby Gavin were alone in their house (a small hut). The three-year-old found matches, accidentally lit one, panicked, and threw it on the bed. Gavin was lying on the end of the bed as the entire bed caught fire. Gavin's legs were badly burned. Mary lost her house and everything she owned, but her children made it out alive. She pulled down the blanket covering Gavin to show us his wounds. I felt a wave of devastation. I just wanted to cry and hold him. One leg was discolored and he had no toes. His burns were starting to heal. His other leg was amputated from the knee down and the doctors had gradually been placing skin grafts on his leg, which took a while because it was so small. They had another month left in the hospital. Mary didn't have money or a house and wasn't sure what she was going to do once Gavin was released. How was she going to pay for her son's medical bills? Despite her situation, she was so hopeful and grateful, saying, "God has blessed me by protecting my children and keeping them alive."

Alison Beale

I fought tears during my entire conversation with her. I figured the least I could do was not cry so I could be hopeful with her. I was so inspired by her hope, her trust in God, and her positivity. After enduring all of that hardship? Knowing that her child's life would be an unimaginable challenge? I found myself sitting there asking God how this could happen. Why did this have to happen to this innocent baby and wonderful woman? This tragic accident would affect not only them, but her other child who lit the match as well. It was an accident that he'd be reminded of every day. While I was sitting there angry with God, she was sitting there thanking God for her blessings. Her attitude was a wake-up call—I had some work to do on my perspective and myself.

We commented that Gavin looked like a happy baby, and she said that it was the three of us who were making him happy. She said she hadn't seen him that happy until we visited. She asked us to visit her again, which we did when we went back to the hospital a couple days later. When Mary saw us she said, "You came back, you came back! You love me and my son."

Earlier that day, Mary had been speaking with a representative from an organization that deals with burn victims. She was hoping they would accept Gavin as a patient and help him. "The acceptance process can be long," she said, but she was praying that it would come through for them. We sat on the bed with Gavin, and she told us again, "He never smiled until you came to see him the other day. He usually doesn't smile because of his pain."

She also said she told her husband that Gavin had American friends now. Mary was so grateful for everything: for us, for God, for her children's lives. One thing I noticed across the board with the hospital patients I met was how grateful and hopeful they were despite their circumstances. Instead of being angry with God, they were thanking Him. Their ability to recognize their blessings even in the worst of situations was inspiring.

Be joyful in hope, patient in affliction, faithful in prayer. Romans 12:12

Mary made it so clear that Kim, Karla and I touched her and Gavin's lives, and that's an amazing thing to know. Spending a little bit of time with them went such a long way. I may not be able to save all of Africa, and the amount of help needed in the world is overwhelming, but this situation is a reminder of the incredible impact I, as one individual, am able to have on people that God places right in front of me.

✳✳✳

The most powerful moment of my life happened on my last day in Haiti. We had finished building Kazi's house and were returning for the blessing of the house by a pastor. Members of the community came to pray together over Kazi's new home. Kazi was overjoyed. She danced around, giving us all hugs and kisses. It was clear to us that we had helped an incredible woman with contagious joy. I can't even put into words the amount of gratitude she showed.

On that trip, I had completely fallen in love with Anderson, a five-year-old boy in the neighborhood. When I first met him, he was so shy that he would barely look at anyone. That quickly changed. He loved the attention we gave him, and he came to hang out with us every day. We had a lot of fun playing with him, and it was hard knowing we'd be leaving him. I had grown so attached to him in such a short amount of time. It hurt to know he'd probably continue to come to Kazi's expecting to see us.

As we all stood around Kazi's home during the blessing, I felt Anderson knew that we wouldn't be coming back so I went over to see him. He jumped into my arms, putting his arms around my neck and burying his face in me. He wouldn't look at anyone. It was then that I knew that he knew we were leaving. It killed me. I tried so hard to hold back my tears, but that proved to be impossible. I started to cry while I was holding him. I am a person who hates being vulnerable, so this was my worst nightmare. I was holding Anderson, so I couldn't cover my face, and I was crying in front of about thirty people. Because I felt vulnerable, I panicked. All I could do was stand there. As a wave of panic ran through me, Kazi came over. I was wearing a tank top with a shirt over it, and she took the bottom of my shirt and wiped my tears. She gave me the biggest hug and just held me. With her on one side of me and Anderson on the other, I was completely engulfed in love. I have never felt more loved, comforted, and safe than I did in that moment. It didn't matter that I hardly knew Kazi. It didn't matter that Kazi and Anderson didn't speak the same language as me. It didn't matter that I came from a completely different lifestyle and background. Love is universal. God's love is universal.

There is neither Jew nor Gentile, neither slave nor free, nor is there male and female, for you are all one in Christ Jesus. Galatians 3:28

Anderson, Kazi, and Wilson live in Haiti and live a completely different life than I do, but they are my family. Mary, Gavin, and all of the wonderful Kenyans I met live across the world, but they are my family. The people I met on these journeys healed me in a way I never knew I needed to be healed.

I went on these mission trips to help those in need of things necessary for survival: food, water, medicine, and shelter. I was able to help provide these things and had great time along the way. Here in the United States, most of us have what we need to survive, but many of us lack what we need to really live. The joy, appreciation, gratitude and love for God, for life, and for all blessings is abundant in Haiti and Kenya. The people I encountered may not have enough food or clothing, but they possess happiness that is unmatched by anything I've experienced or witnessed in the U.S. I am so grateful that I got to take some of that joy home with me. I still get caught up in the minuscule problems that come along with daily life, but I see things differently now. I am different than I was before I went to Haiti and Kenya. There's no way you can experience that kind of love and not come back with radically different perspectives, dispositions and priorities.

It's easy to be selfish and to act with our own interests in mind. It's easy to be complacent and comfortable. It's easy to live in our own bubbles and ignore the fact that there are people in need — whether they are in our community, in our country, or on the other side of the world. By living a self-serving life, however, it's also easy to be unsatisfied and to always want more. My hands are by no means 100% clean of this selfish lifestyle, despite my experiences that have taught me to live otherwise. I am not saying we need to forget about our wants and needs, nor am I passing judgment. But, if there is one thing I've learned, it is that we should live for others. We ought to be conscious of the needs of others, and we should strive to do everything in our power to help where help is needed. Just because something is not a problem in our immediate lives does not mean it's not a problem. We have to show love and we have to care, even when it's hard, inconvenient, or uncomfortable. We are all broken people, but God heals and we can heal one another on an earthly level as well. We are called to go and love, a simple calling, just not always an easy one. But by living for others, I believe you'll find the happiness and satisfaction you're constantly trying to find by living for yourself. I know I have.

Alison Beale

Alison Beale

A Case of Mistaken Identity

Jean-Ann Cooper

Trust in the Lord with all your heart and do not lean on your own understanding. In all your ways acknowledge Him, and He will make your paths straight. Proverbs 3:5-6 NIV

For years, I lived a life of mistaken identity, trying to define who I was by any other means than finding my identity in my Lord and Savior, Jesus Christ. Had I prayed Proverbs 3:5-6 into my life at an early age, the story I am about to tell you may have been much different.

From the time I was a little girl, I had a people-pleasing streak as wide as a six-lane highway with no off ramp. Being accommodating, unconditionally loving and accepting of others is the right thing to do, but it can also lead to a path of ruin if we are not careful. In my case, it resulted in a life of mistaken identity. My life was defined by the man I was with, the job title I held, and the size of my paycheck.

Don't get me wrong, my people-pleasing skills worked to my advantage countless times. I took great pleasure in being known as the "go-to girl." Whenever there was a committee to form, a project to complete or an ugly task to be done, the battle cry was, "Just ask Jean-Ann. She'll do it!" People trusted me, and that trust made me feel needed and appreciated and loved.

I possessed an odd combination of strong leadership skills with an unbridled willingness to be led around as if I had a big brass ring in my nose! I was strong and self-reliant, for sure. It was easy for me to stand firm and say, "Oh, hell no!" about an issue I disagreed with, but I did not have a clue about how to turn down a simple request.

I remember my first coed dance like it was yesterday. I was in seventh grade at Palo Verde Elementary School in Phoenix, Arizona. For several weeks leading up to the big dance, all the kids in my class had mandatory dance lessons on Thursdays after school. The boys learned how to ask a girl to dance, and the girls learned the proper way to accept their invitation.

The dance instructor looked like a drill sergeant and had a personality to match. She wore clunky shoes and pointy glasses. She wore her hair up in a bun that was so tight; her eyes slanted up at the corners. She was deadly serious when it came to teaching our gangly group of twelve-year-olds the waltz and the foxtrot. None of us liked the lessons much, but the mere idea of dancing with a boy had my girlfriends and me giddy with excitement!

The big night finally arrived. I loved my white dress with big red and pink California poppies on the skirt and a wide pink ribbon sash for the belt. My white Mary Jane patent leather shoes were perfect, and Mom curled my hair just the way I liked it.

Before leaving the house, my Mom sat me down, held my hands and said she wanted to share some advice on how to make sure I had a great time at the dance that night. She was my best friend. I trusted her, so of course, I could not wait to hear her secret.

"When a boy, any boy, asks you do dance, you need to accept his invitation."

"Any boy? MOM!" I said.

"Yes, any boy. I don't care if he is tall, short, fat, skinny, cute or not. If that young man has mustered up the courage to ask you to dance, you owe it to him to say yes. If you dance with the first boy who asks you, I promise, you will dance all night."

Mom was right. After accepting the first few invitations, I danced to nearly every song and had the time of my life! It was years later that I realized my mom was not as interested in my enjoying the dance as much as she was teaching me the value of being considerate, inclusive and welcoming. She wanted me to be attractive, not just pretty.

My parents intended to raise my brothers and me to attract the good things and good people in life by being kind, open, honest and trustworthy. I remember countless times when I was leaving the house to go to a high school dance or a party; Mom would call out, "Don't worry about being the prettiest girl, be the most attractive girl and you will have a great night!" She wanted people to be drawn to me for all the right reasons—for who I was not how I looked. She wanted me to attract others by being a magnet, not a model.

Sadly, the unintended consequence of the magnet vs. model concept was that I never learned how to say no. To anything. Or to anyone. I mean, there could be red flags flying, and warning sirens blaring in the background, and still, I would say, "Yes! Of course! Absolutely! Happy to!" Nothing got in the way of my trying to please everyone.

And so it began…

After dating a handsome young man for a few months, he asked me to marry him and totally swept me off my feet. Of course, I said yes! Why wouldn't I? He professed his undying love for me and wanted to be my husband and the father of my children….SWOON!

Then came the wedding day. I was dressed in a beautiful white gown and clinging to my father's arm in the back of the church waiting for the wedding procession to begin when my dad turned to me and smiled. I smiled back as the tears streamed down my face.

"Honey," my dad said, "you do not have to do this."

All I said was, "Daddy, start walking."

I could not bear the thought of leaving my future husband at the altar! Moreover, disappointing all of our guests was out of the question. I worried more about what other people would think than what a failed marriage would do to my life.

We had only been married a few months and were still giddy newlyweds when I unexpectedly came home early from work one day. He'd recently been laid off from his construction job, and to say he was flipped out about our finances would be an understatement.

Neither of us made much money, and without his paycheck, we were at risk of losing the house his father helped us buy.

I walked in and found him sitting at our rickety little kitchen table. A small scale, a mound of grayish powder and a bag of little balloons was on the table in front of him. I immediately knew this was not good. Or normal. Or legal. He said his uncle was paying him good money to measure doses of heroin into single dose balloon packets to sell.

I have no recollection of exactly what I said to him, but I do remember it being loud and ugly. I do remember how shocked he was that I was so angry. Sure we had smoked pot a few times, but heroin? No way! He stood his ground by saying we needed the money to pay our mortgage, righteously proclaiming it was his job, as the man of the house, to take care of our finances. I packed and left that weekend.

When I left the marriage, I did not tell my parents or my brothers the truth about the heroin. I was too embarrassed, and I knew they would be horrified! They pleaded with me to stay in the marriage and do all I could to work things out. They begged me to talk with the Priest who had married us, but I had no interest in telling the truth or lying to Father John. I told my family there was no way I was going to stay in the marriage and I was filing for divorce immediately. End of discussion.

My parents were fabulous people and completely committed to their Catholic faith. We were super involved in our parish life, volunteering and faithfully attending Mass, catechism classes and holy days of obligation. My aunt was a Nun; my dad was the head usher of our parish and Mom was the head sacristan. Mom and I spent most Saturdays polishing communion chalices and ironing the Priest's robes and the altar cloths. When I got older, I sang in the choir and was active in the Catholic Youth Organization. The Church was the centerpiece of our lives, and I loved it.

My divorce meant I was excommunicated and could no longer take part in the sacraments. On Sunday mornings, it was glaringly obvious that I was the black sheep of a good Catholic family. I knew it had to be a terrible embarrassment to my family when, instead of taking communion from the Priest at the altar, I stayed kneeling in the pew, eyes cast down hoping against hope no one would judge me. The shame nearly consumed me.

Our divorce was final a few days short of what would have been our first anniversary. My twenty-first birthday was the following month, which meant I was finally old enough to drink...legally, that is. It was the mid-70s, and disco was all the rage. I loved going to bars and dancing to songs by Donna Summer, The Bee Gees, and Diana Ross. To be honest, I was wildly fond of the numbing effects of alcohol on my shame-filled brain.

I had only been single a short time when I met a charming man at a local discotheque. He was a little older and was divorced. He had a young son, and I fell head over heels in love with both of them. We were married five months later. Why? Because he said he loved me. I would have the opportunity to be a mom, even if it was only part-time, and I hoped being a wife with a family meant I would no longer feel like a divorced, excommunicated loser.

I know! I am rolling my eyes, too!

He was a journeyman carpenter and a good provider. He loved his beer...lots and lots of beer. Beer seemed pretty tame to me, considering the heroin incident. At least getting drunk was something we could do together. My husband was a barrel of fun after a few beers and, for reasons too lengthy to delve into, he had a bad case of pent-up, smoldering, nasty, hateful anger.

On some nights he would drink too much, and that anger would rear its ugly head. On a regular basis, he would get rough with me, push or slap me and at times, shove me against the wall while he screamed and yelled obscenities. It was bad, but not bad enough to leave. The big payoff came the next morning when he would wake me up with sweet kisses and bring me breakfast in bed. He would apologize, beg for forgiveness and promise to treat me like a princess from that day forward. He would profess his undying love adding that he could not imagine life without me. I learned, firsthand, why battered women stay with their abusers. The intensity of the love after the battle can be extremely addictive.

One night, he was very drunk and completely outraged, which was a horrible combination. An ugly argument escalated far beyond name-calling, pushing and shoving, and I ended up with a giant black eye, lots of bruises and a few cracked ribs. With obvious physical wounds, I was no longer able to hide the abuse from my friends, co-workers, and family. Everyone blamed him, but I know I played a part.

It would be easy to put all the blame on husbands #1 and #2. However, the truth was hard to deny. I was the common denominator which left me no choice but to take responsibility for my role in the bad decisions and disgusting behavior. So there I was, signing divorce papers again at twenty-four years old. Once again steeped in shame and vowing never to marry again.

It was abundantly clear that I sucked at the "wife thing" and since I figured I would be single the rest of my life, I needed a job. No, I needed more than a job, I needed a career and a good one at that. In those days, that meant dark suits, pantyhose, and closed toed shoes. I decided if I was going to go through all that trouble (especially the pantyhose thing!) I was determined to make real money.

By the time I was thirty, a combination of hard work, a few calculated risks and lots of luck helped me land a great job at a top radio station in town. With a good paycheck and a manager's title, I felt worthy of respect again.

Fully trusting in my own abilities and leaning on my own understanding was finally starting to work out for me. Or so it seemed.

Several years later, my life was on solid ground, and my career was in full bloom. I broke the promise I had made to myself and married again. This time I married a man ten years older with a high profile position. It was the third marriage for both of us. I loved him but wasn't "in love" with him, if that makes any sense at all. The relationship seemed more mature than any of my other relationships. I was oddly comforted that we were great friends and cared for each other deeply, but weren't crazy in love. It felt safe.

We married on a Friday morning surrounded by a few close friends and family members. That night, we celebrated in grand style with a big party with family and friends at our home. The food was excellent, and the cocktails were flowing like a rushing river! Everyone was having a great time.

At the end of the evening, I stood in the doorway of my beautiful new home saying goodbye to the last group of friends and was completely overwhelmed by how happy I was. The weeks leading up to the wedding had been exciting and hectic as we wrapped up all the loose ends for a perfect ceremony and a fabulous party. With all of that behind us, I was eager to spend the next several days with the love of my life, relaxing, enjoying each other and planning our new life together.

The house was quiet, and I remember thinking it was funny that only twelve hours into the marriage, I had lost track of my groom. He was quite the social butterfly, so I assumed he was walking friends to their cars. I went into the backyard to take in the fresh, crisp air and saw two shadows near the far end of the pool. As I drew a few steps closer, I realized it was husband and my dear friend, Pam. Kissing... on my wedding day! They were embarrassed and blamed it on the alcohol. Pam rushed out of the house in tears, and I never heard from her again. My husband and I never talked about it. I never brought it up because, in my heart, I knew he would apologize profusely, and say anything he needed to say to get me to drop the subject, so I figured, why bother? It was just easier to let it go.

Over the years we were married, he had other women I knew about and heard countless rumors about more, but to be fair, neither one of us honored our vows the way we should have. We did not argue or fight. We just co-existed. I was hoping our move to Dallas a few years later would give us the new start we desperately needed, but after six years, the marriage ended. We just didn't love each other enough.

While my third marriage was crumbling, my career was taking off like a rocket. Being single again meant my job was the top priority of my life. I quickly learned that if you are successful in the corporate ranks, having three divorces under your belt is no big deal. In fact, it may have helped me earn a reputation of being tough and thick-skinned, which worked to my advantage in the male-dominated television industry.

Life was great! I lived on the seventeenth floor of a high-rise condo in the prestigious Turtle Creek area of Dallas. I had a hefty six-figure salary and a brand new pair of perky boobs. I felt like I was at the top of my game!

Why in the world would I be remotely tempted to do as the Proverb suggested and acknowledge God in all my ways when I was the one who worked so hard to get here?

Out of the blue one day, a woman named Jo called me. She was married to one of my competitors, and though we'd met a few times at industry functions, I did not know her well. She said, "You have been on my mind so much lately. I think the Holy Spirit has been prompting me to call you."

My first thought? What has she been smoking?

She told me she had a one-on-one ministry and mentored women in their walk of faith using a Bible study called "Discovering Jesus." She wanted to know if I was open to going through the study with her. *NO!!* I screamed silently in my head, but because I did not want to hurt her feelings, what came out of my mouth was, "Sure Jo, I would love to do that."

Jo's love for the Lord was very real and critically important to her. She had been a longtime follower of Jesus and loved Him more than anyone I had ever known. She spoke as if He was someone she knew personally. Jo gently, but boldly shared her faith and God's love with all who would listen. It was unbelievable how she accepted me, warts and all, and loved me unconditionally.

The study revealed that God had a plan and a purpose for my life and better yet, that I did not have to work at it. God's grace, I learned, is His free and unmerited favor. Up until then, grace was nothing more than the rote prayer we said before dinner.

Before studying with Jo, I had never even cracked open a Bible. Growing up, we had a Family Bible. It was a giant, dusty black book with gold edges on the pages. It lived on the top shelf of the hall closet. I do not remember any of us ever reading it, but I do remember it being used to keep records of important family events. Whenever a new baby was born, someone got baptized or married or died, the Bible came off the top shelf of the hall closet, the event recorded and then back on the shelf it went until the next noteworthy event.

Over the next few months, Jo and I would meet at my house or a nearby restaurant to go over the week's study. Jo's easy way of mentoring provided a safe place for me. For the first time in my life, I was not shy about asking silly questions about faith, Jesus, His disciples, or any other topic. Jo's mentoring style made me hungry to dig deeper and deeper into His Word.

In March 2000, I attended a weekend event called "A Walk to Emmaus" at a camp near Lake Lavon just north of Dallas. Over the course of three days, I heard various speakers give talks and share their powerful testimonies of victory and redemption. We all participated in hilarious skits, art projects, praise and worship and the most incredible communion service I have ever experienced.

After finishing our group activities on Saturday night, I took a walk alone by the lake and sat on a bench under a sprawling oak tree. It was a new moon that night and the only lights shining were the stars overhead and the lights from the cabins off in the distance. It was so peaceful and quiet; it was unnerving.

For years, I avoided being alone and quiet, afraid of where my regrets and shame would take me. That night was different. I knew God loved me, no matter what. I was tired of being in charge of my life and screwing it up over and over and over again. I tried to be a good person and do the right thing, but no matter what I did or how hard I worked at it, I always fell short. I was a total mess.

I sat alone in the dark and cried like I have never cried before or since. I have no idea how long I sat on that bench, but that night, I broke down, gave it all up, and surrendered my life to my Lord, Jesus. It was on a rickety old bench under an oak tree where I found my true identity.

That was the first time I realized that I was His beloved. I was not worthy of His sacrifice, but He gave up His life for me so that I would be free. At that moment, I knew that He had been waiting for me all along, that His promises were real and that He would never leave me. That night, He became my Lord and my Savior.

Over the next year, I joined a women's study at a nearby Bible church. The more I learned, the more I talked with friends and family about what I was learning about Jesus and how His grace was an amazing gift that He wanted us all to enjoy. I was a Jesus loving Bible thumper and proud of it!

God works in mysterious ways, so I doubt it was by chance that my best friend Susie was Jewish and had never been in a Bible study either. God is a funny guy that way! He puts the right people in your life at the right time for the right reasons! Amen? Anyhooo, we decided we would get together on Monday nights, share a bottle of wine and dive into God's Word. I loved those nights! Having a friend by my side on my faith journey was truly one of God's greatest gifts.

The more Susie and I studied, the more we shared with our friends. Before long, there were thirteen of us meeting each week! We did not know much about the Bible, but we knew where the Lifeway store was. We found helpful clerks to direct us to studies, DVDs, books and workbooks by Beth Moore, Priscilla Shirer, and others.

Our "Happy Hour Bible Study Group" is an amazing group of women and we love each other like family. We have faithfully used Scripture and offered prayer support to each other in good times and in bad. We have danced at each other's weddings, and have been brought to our knees by divorces, miscarriages, scary health issues and spotty employment. We have welcomed newborn babies and grandbabies and have grieved the death of parents, family and friends. In the summer of 2007, we tragically lost one of our own to ovarian cancer.

This group has loved me and held me accountable. My relationship with each and every one of them is unique. I have always joked (though I am deadly serious!) that without them, I would be robbing 7-Elevens! They are my tribe, my posse, and my sisters-in-Christ. They have enriched my walk of faith, and I will lovingly cling to them forever.

In my walk—more like my stumble—of faith, some incredible men and women have come alongside me with much-needed support and encouragement. Steve Smith truly is my brother-in-Christ. He has gifted me with countless books and deep, meaningful talks. It was people like Steve who helped guide me and not try to fix me. He openly shared his struggles with me and, because of that, earned the right to hear mine. He is an excellent example of the kind of supportive friend I want to be for others.

I am blessed to be married again. Yep, this is #4 for me but who's counting? It is by the grace of God that Bob and I have been married since 1996, many more years than my three previous marriages combined! He is the spiritual head of our household and the greatest guy who ever drew breath! Even though he is incredibly handsome and my heart skips a beat every time he walks into the room, the most attractive thing about him is his love for the Lord.

One of the many fringe benefits of being married to Bob is becoming part of his family. I never did have my own kids, but I have giant stretch marks on my heart from loving Bob's. He has an amazing daughter and two terrific sons. I love them and their spouses like my own and doubt that I could ever birth any better! The icing on the cake is our five adorable grandchildren, who call me "Boo" which, in my humble opinion, is the coolest grandma name on the planet!

I love being Bob's wife, but the foundation of my identity is not in being Mrs. Robert L. Cooper. Today I know who I am and Whom I serve. I am a beloved child of God, and I have willingly surrendered my life to Him. I am blessed beyond measure to have an unwavering faith in my Lord and Savior, Jesus Christ.

Scripture tells me that [1]*I am God's masterpiece*—without Him, I know that I am nothing more than a stick figure. He promises to [2]*never leave me, nor forsake me. And* [3]*when troubles come, I am assured* [4]*I can do all things through Christ, who strengthens me.*

I pray none of you ever allow the enemy to confuse you like he did me all those years. I pray you never fall into the trap of defining who you are by your spouse or significant other, by your success or failure, the house you live in, the car your drive, your family of origin or even your adorable children. None of us can afford to allow that to happen. We are all children of the One, True, Living and Loving God!

My dear friend and first Bible study partner, Jo, promised me there would come a day when I would thank God for all the pain and struggle of those difficult years. Once again I thought, what has she been smoking? However, today, I can say that Jo was right! Those trials and troubles helped me draw me closer to Him. Without them, I would have missed the joy of an intimate relationship with Jesus and the confidence that comes with knowing [5]*my sins are forgiven.*

For too many years I hid the story of my failed marriages and thought of myself as a three-time loser. But [6]*by His grace through faith*, I have come to know that [7]*I am a new creation in Christ* and [8]*His Royal Heir.* Imagine that!

Today, I teach, mentor and coach women who are incarcerated or recently released from prison. I am blessed to share the Gospel each time I speak at a local church or women's retreat. Like Jo's gift to me, I hope my teaching and mentoring style offers them all a safe place to land. I pray they see only love and acceptance in my eyes. Moreover, I pray the Lord empties me and fills me up with his love and grace so that I can pour it out on these women who, like me, so desperately need Him.

Today I pray my life verse, Proverbs 3:5-6, in a personal way— *Heavenly Father, I trust You with all my heart, help me to remember always to lean on You rather than my own understanding. I pray to honor You in all my ways and to allow You, and only You, to direct my path.*

Without You, Father, I am nothing. With You, I have everything I could ever hope for or imagine. Thank you for saving me from myself. Thank you for taking control of my out-of-control life. [9]*Your yoke is easy, and Your burden is light. I am forever grateful for the* [10]*unmerited grace You constantly shower over me.*

You, Christ Jesus, Are [11]*Awesome!*

Are you living a life of mistaken identity? Are you still trying to do this life on your own? Are you tired of the daily grind and the burden of carrying a heavy load? If so, I would encourage you to seek the Lord with all your heart. It is time to stop fighting the battle that He has already won on your behalf. Maybe, just maybe, it is time to put your trust in Him. He desperately wants a relationship with you, and take it from a big fat sinner like me, we all desperately need Him! My prayers will be with you as you journey on a path to the throne. It may be a little scary at first, but I promise you will not be sorry.

He is waiting. Are you willing?

[1] Ephesians 2:10
[2] Dueteronomy 31:6
[3] John 16:33
[4] Philippians 4:13
[5] Psalm 103:12
[6] Ephesians 2:8
[7] 2 Corinthians 5:17
[8] Romans 8:17
[9] Matthew 11:29-30
[10] 2 Peter 1:2
[11] Psalm 47:2

Jean-Ann Cooper

Just Like Me

Courtney Diehl

My mother and father did not attend church, and I was not raised with any particular faith. We were not atheists, but we just did not practice any spirituality or religion in my home. Both of my parents had been raised in families where religion and God were used as weapons, and both knew the church only as a place of hypocrisy and superstition. Therefore, the church was a place to be avoided and mistrusted, and I grew up with a deep suspicion of all things religious. I felt disdainful of people who attended church, viewing them as brainwashed, and as non-thinkers.

I wasn't exactly a ripe candidate for coming to embrace faith and love God. But God is persistent, and as our creator, knows our inner workings far better than we do. What better way to get me into church than to place a cute young man who was a devout Christian in my path, but was also fairly worldly. We were both living in Colorado, and were both hard partying ski bums. I developed a major crush on him, but was baffled by his persistent attachment to church and to God. He was a Pentecostal Christian, and I remember thinking that it was something he'd get over if he could just see another point of view.

He didn't get over the church nonsense, but I found myself liking him more and more. We lived in different towns, and it occurred to me that if he thought I was a good Christian too, then he'd fall madly in love with me, and we'd live happily ever after. So I pulled out the phone book in Fort Collins, CO, and looked up churches in the yellow pages. They were listed by denomination, so I decided to attend every church corresponding to Pentecostals until I found one that I liked. I'd start with the A's and work my way down.

From Pentecostal, I branched out into Assemblies of God churches. Some seemed more traditional, while others told you to burn your television and warned that *Cosmopolitan* magazine was inspired by Satan. I kept attending new churches, week after week, but was starting to despair of finding one that I could relate to, and I was finding myself getting more and more critical of the people and the sermons. Out of fear, I became determined to find ammunition to boost my position that churches were nothing more than hypocritical, creepy places.

With my attitude, it's no wonder I couldn't find a church that I liked. But as hard as I looked to find the negative points of each place, I couldn't help but notice one common theme. All of the people at these churches seemed to be part of a tight, supportive group, and they also seemed happy. There was a sense of peace and a joy about them that I could not understand.

I believed that I was not worthy of receiving peace and joy. Whatever this God stuff might have been about, I was permanently excluded, and I got angrier and became more isolated. When the pastor prayed, or asked the new believers to accept Jesus, I resisted so hard that I'd leave with a headache. No God and no church would want me. I was too cynical, and had seen and done some fairly bad things in my life. If people in these churches knew the truth about my past behavior, they'd probably throw me out.

I stuck to my old tactic of isolation. Since I stayed off to the side, made no effort to interact with anyone, and then fled as soon as the service was over, I wasn't connecting anywhere, and I thought this strengthened my argument about how dreadful these church people were, and how they snubbed outsiders. I couldn't see any connection with my behavior.

One Sunday, weary of traipsing in and out of strange churches, and tired of feeling "rejected" by people, I'd reached the "T" section in the Fort Collins phone book. Timberline Church. My cynicism was at its peak, and I resolved that after this church, my experiment was ending, and I was giving up for good. Forget the cute boy. I was done.

By now I was fairly used to entering strange churches and keeping a safe distance, and I got a cup of coffee and took a seat by myself in the very last pew, closest to the exit. The first thing I noticed was people wearing jeans and t-shirts instead of prim church clothes. There seemed to be several bikers scattered around the pews, and I saw some tattoos and ponytails on a few men. The women were dressed similarly, casually, and everyone moved around the church in a friendly manner, greeting people. I assumed everyone was only talking with their friends, and was caught off guard when someone came over to me and shook my hand and introduced themselves.

I was reluctant to get caught in a conversation, so I pretended I had to use the restroom and fled. When the coast was clear, I returned to my safe perch in the back and the service started. Soon, I was surprised to find myself really listening and taking the sermon to heart. No pastor I'd ever met had preached a message like this one. Pastor Dary was talking about people just like me, with a yearning for God but with a hard, cynical heart. He spoke about how God looks for the lost and the broken and when they turn to him, he rejoices that they've come home. He said something I've never ever forgotten- that the opposite of cynicism was hope, and that hope was the beginning of faith.

It was a real message, for real people, and at the end of it, he blew my mind completely when he explained that Jesus walked among the thieves, the tax collectors, the criminals and built relationships by bringing hope, encouragement and acceptance to those not used to receiving it. Jesus didn't sit in a church with Sunday-curled hair and Sunday clothes and a smug expression on his face shaking a reprimanding finger sternly at sinners. He was out there in the mud and the stink, reaching and loving others who needed him. People just like me.

I was wiping away tears at the end of the service, and made my usual quick bolt for the door. But the pastor had discovered my hiding place and had made a beeline for me and before I could escape, I found myself shaking hands and talking with this amazing man who had just ripped my heart apart.

What I didn't know back then was that pastors cleverly study the back row, as people just like me tend to try to hide there. What I also didn't know back then was that I was hardly as unique as I'd imagined myself to be. There were plenty of other people out there who saw the world exactly as I did, a concept which had never occurred to me. I was suffering from a severe case of "terminal uniqueness," a disease of the spirit, and that day at the Timberline Church, my self-imposed isolation from God and from other people began to shatter. I was no longer alone.

The process of re-entry took years. I was baptized at Timberline Church, and attended regularly for two years. I then started veterinary school in St. Kitts, an island in the West Indies. Church there tended to last over three hours, and I tried to attend every Sunday but was defeated by the heat, the flies, and the rock hard seats. I moved to Minnesota where I finished my schooling, and then to New York for a veterinary internship, drifting further from the church. I returned to Colorado to set up private practice and found myself returning to my old ways and to my old crowd of hard partying friends.

Luckily, the changes which had been forged in the old days at Timberline Church, had shifted my heart, and I could not return fully to that lifestyle. I was no longer going to be satisfied with the partying and the shallow friendships. I knew in my soul there was something a lot better out there, and I knew God was on my side, even though I hadn't been actively participating in a relationship with him. I kept him at bay, telling myself I was far too busy with my career, and since I was a believer and I'd been baptized, that was enough. Surely no more work on the God-part was needed.

I gave up the party lifestyle for good and settled into a steady relationship which would result in marriage. We moved around some more before settling in Steamboat Springs, Colorado. A vet colleague invited us to church one day, and suddenly I realized that I hadn't set foot in one since St. Kitts, many years ago with the heat and the flies. My husband was out of town, so I went to Steamboat Christian Center with my vet friend, and quickly realized that I belonged there. I felt that

God was welcoming me back with joy and not with any judgement, and Pastor Troy reminded me a lot of Pastor Dary from the Timberline days. The congregation was similar to Timberline Church, and as I began to settle in, I realized that I'd been mourning the loss of the first church where I'd ever fit in. I didn't know that there were other churches out there like Timberline. For people just like me.

My faith and relationship with God have blossomed since that day. Pastor Troy talks about a "God-shaped hole" in the human heart which creates a vacuum if not filled by God. We were created to be in fellowship with God and with people on earth, and if we're not connecting, we become angry and hurt and devoid of hope. Over time, anger, hurt and lost hope harden into cynicism.

I was baptized again, to renew my commitment to God and to the church, and in my second year with SCC, I joined the jail ministry team. There was a blurb in the church bulletin about the ministry, and something about it appealed to me. There was an excitement about stepping out in faith and entering a jail, but there was something else drawing me to the ministry.

It's been four years now, and slowly I've come to understand why I'm there. I'm fairly fluent in "broken and lost" and I understand having strongholds of shame, isolation, guilt and cynicism. I can only break those down by connecting with God and with others just like me. Every week I leave the jail with something new to think about. I can't hold onto my peace and serenity unless I'm giving it away.

It's a daily process, this relationship with God, and it just gets better with time. When I live in close fellowship with my creator, slowly but surely, he changes my heart and renews my mind. I don't think it's too crazy to hope that someday, I'll become just like him.

Courtney Diehl

It's Never Too Late

Michele Dudas

What is "normal?" When I started to write my story for this book, I thought I had led a fairly normal life. But as I peeled back the layers of the years and recalled the events of my life, I realized that many things were and are still now far from normal, whatever that is. What I do know is that I have lived a life of ups and downs, happiness and hurts, selflessness and selfishness, and trying to be the best I can be—usually through my own efforts.

Mine is a story of finding true peace and joy despite circumstances and of letting all the little daily frustrations and challenges serve as practice for when the big stuff hits.

Born in the mid-1940s on the front edge of the Baby Boomers, my formative years were in the 50s and early 60s. This meant transitioning from the ideal fantasy world of an Ozzie and Harriet perfect-family lifestyle into and through the hippie generation. As was typical of most Baby Boomers, my father was the bread winner, and my mother was a housewife. Dad owned the laundry in town and was known as a "pillar" of the community. As was true of many little girls, he was my hero. Both of my parents were only children which meant both sets of our grandparents were a big part of our lives. Every holiday was spent together, and we kids visited them often. During my grade school years I especially loved spending weekends at my mom's parents, drinking root beer floats while watching late TV on Friday nights. We played outside among the berry bushes by the pond, swung in the hammock tied between the fruit trees, picked through the real trash dump right on the property, and ate the sweetest corn I've ever tasted from Grandma's small cornfield. My Grandma Welch was a huge influence in my life. She planted in me some of the first seeds for Jesus as she set an example of consistently attending a Bible-believing church and took me with her on occasion.

Vacations were few and far between and most often consisted of road trips to historical sites my dad liked to visit. We had a dog and the nicest house in the neighborhood. Money was always tight, but my dad could fix anything and make it look good. We had a manicured lawn and drove second hand Cadillac convertibles, so most of my friends thought we were rich!

I loved school, and learning came easy. I graduated third in my high school class and was voted "Most Popular Girl" my senior year. As a cheerleader I was looked up to by my peers. Making friends also came easily, and I was involved in many activities. I sang in and played piano for the choir, appeared in school plays, and participated in or led many academic activities. I did well in anything I chose to do. Later in life, however, I discovered that what I didn't succeed at was developing persistence; if I couldn't succeed at something immediately, I just moved on to something else.

Our family attended a local Christian church. The pastor was a good friend of my dad's, and my dad led the choir for several years. I remember how proud I was seeing him directing the choir, playing the piano, and singing. I can still recall one day in Sunday school when the pastor paid his annual visit to teach the kids, and he asked if anyone knew what a prophet was. Confidently raising my hand I responded, "It's what my daddy makes in his laundry business." That story got a good laugh at the next Lions Club lunch meeting where both the pastor and my dad met each week.

When I was in Junior High School, my parents stopped going to church. I never knew why. Mom and Dad both passed away almost thirty years ago, and there are many things I wish I had asked them. But things were different in that generation, and we didn't communicate much about feelings and decisions. Kids were expected to respect adult decisions and to not question why. So they began to take us to church but not go themselves. And I, being an adolescent and becoming more interested in things other than church, found a reason to stop going. I had heard that a black family had moved into town and wanted to attend our church. The powers that be in the church had supposedly told them they weren't welcome, that they should attend the church where the other black people went. I didn't know the word hypocrisy back then, but I never did see a black person in our church, and it didn't seem right to me. I believed that God loved us all, regardless of skin color. And so I quit going to church. I don't remember ever telling anyone why, and I don't remember my parents ever pushing me to go again. Church simply wasn't a part of my life then or for many years. *But I did believe in God.*

In college I became a different person, almost as if rebelling against a too-rigid upbringing. But that hadn't been the case. I had been loved and popular and had been brought up to be honest and decent and considerate. So, while I still studied hard in preparation for my chosen profession Speech Pathology in a new area of Special Education, at Ohio University, and became involved again in activities, my morality and sexuality went down the tubes. My sexual partners were many and my serious relationships few. A sixteen year addiction to smoking began the moment I set foot in my freshman dormitory. Alcohol and partying, along with studying, became my life for four years. I never got in trouble, never had an auto accident, and my parents were pretty much oblivious to my lifestyle. *Perhaps that's why I still believed in God. He was watching over me.*

My twenties, thirties, and most of my forties brought three decades of seemingly responsible living and success in my careers. I had moved to California for my first husband to finish graduate school at UC Berkeley, and that's where I stayed for the next thirty years. After a successful twenty-year career in Speech Pathology, I was burned out. So I did the most natural thing that anyone with a Masters' in education would do—opened an espresso bar in the small town just north of Santa Cruz where we lived. Again, I had a wonderful career for ten years that I absolutely loved, but my marital relationships were another story!

During these decades I gave birth to my daughter and raised a stepson and was divorced three (yes, I said three!) times. My lifestyle was different with each marriage. In the first union, climbing the corporate ladder was important, and my life included alcohol, recreational drugs, and extra-marital affairs. The marriage ended after seven years.

A control freak came into my life when I married for the second time. I struggled with many episodes of moral questioning as it was the era of "free love" in the 1970s. What did marriage mean to me and my husband? Our marriage lasted only two years. When I look back, perhaps God was tugging at me through my questioning. I struggled between doing right and doing what my husband demanded. The greatest blessing from this marriage was the birth of my daughter Ali, my only child. I raised her as a single mom until I entered into my third marriage.

My third husband was a gentle and passive man with a son who was the same age as my daughter. We raised our two kids together as a family unit until both were out of high school. During the years I was with him I was constantly searching for something that seemed to be missing. With time, I have come to realize that I was trying to fill a God-shaped hole in my heart. Trying to find that fulfillment through gurus, table tipping and channeling spirits, various healing teachings, and New-Age churches resulted in only temporary peace. This search eventually pulled us apart, and our marriage dissolved after eight years as he became more distant, less responsive, and much less responsible. *I continued to believe in God, but I now see that what was missing was a relationship with Him.*

My real decade of change came in my fifties, and led me to the path I am on now. My present husband, Dick, and I had grown up together in that small town in northeastern Ohio and had been good friends all through school. We had reconnected at our twentieth year class reunion, getting together with our old "gang" and rehashing fond memories. Eleven years after that reunion both Dick and I were divorced, and he found my business card while cleaning out his desk, called me, and the rest is history. (Twenty years later, and knowing him as I do now, I really do believe that Dick kept a business card for eleven years among everything else he kept in his desk!) A long-distance relationship ensued between Vermont and California for three years. I was ready to leave California, and we made the decision to get married.

Dick was a Christian, as were most of his friends and business associates. It's important to note that at this time, even through all my marital and lifestyle challenges, *I still believed in God.* Everyone I met through Dick welcomed me with open arms, accepting me for who I was, and showing me simply through the example of their lives who Jesus was. Meanwhile, God continued to tug at that hole in my heart because He knew it could only be filled with Jesus Himself. And then He brought me into an environment in which people demonstrated His love and the impact it makes in someone's daily life.

In September, 1994 just five days before my fiftieth birthday, at the Sunday morning non-denominational church service during a business conference, I accepted Jesus Christ as my Lord and Savior. My life has not been the same since.

What did it mean for me to be "saved?" What changed?

- I began to devour the Bible to learn from God's Word what He wanted for me and began to have amazing "aha" moments where I knew He was speaking directly to me.
- I learned morals, His morals. That meant no relative truths, no situational ethics. Truth is truth, and God has declared what it is in His Word, the Holy Bible.
- I understood there truly is an enemy. Satan is not some nebulous force in the atmosphere, but a being of great power who wants us to do evil and to disobey God.
- I quit struggling to obey His commands, as I let Him work in my heart. I do not have idols above Him. I love my neighbor and do not lust, covet, lie, steal, or murder. I let Him work out His revenge with those I feel have harmed me.
- I learned to forgive those who I feel have committed wrongs against me. I also learned that my God has forgiven me for the many wrongs I committed against Him.

Yes, my life has gone through dramatic change since Christ came into my life and my heart. You see, most of my life *I believed in God.* I prayed to Him. I believed He was the creator of everything and that He sent His Son Jesus Christ to save us from our sins. I believed all that. But I hadn't accepted Christ as my *personal* Savior and Lord. My acceptance has been a gift that has made all the difference. I am not just a changed person. I am a new creation, and I love who I am and who I continue to become.

Dick and I have been married for twenty years, and what a life I'm living! It is a God-blessed, love-filled, never-boring, always-amazing life. We moved to the western slope of the Rocky Mountains in Colorado several years ago to be near my daughter and her family, allowing for a spiritual as well as geographical closeness. I believe that God wanted Dick and me here because I was to be a spiritual influence for Ali and her family. I had provided her with little spiritual upbringing, to include Jesus and who He is. It was time to share my life with Jesus in it with my family. An unexpected blessing confirmed this for me when my eight year old granddaughter asked me to do a Bible study with her. We have continued this on and off for over three years and now will be including some of her friends. What a joy it is to watch her learn God's Word and apply it to her daily life. It's an experience I never imagined I would be having. But God knew!

I do not live a glamorous life filled with outdoor sports, concerts, parties, weekend trips, and multiple homes, as is typical of many people in this area where we live; but I am living in a beautiful environment—spiritually, emotionally, and physically. I am content. It is nothing short of remarkable to be walking through life with my family and my other Christian families. I see their strengths and weaknesses as well as my own, and we grow and mature together in God's grace and mercy and love.

I used to catch myself feeling envious of others' apparently blessed lives. But I now know in my heart that envy only sees the surface. I understand that sometimes material comforts also come with great sorrows, greater than I have ever known. I would not trade my life for theirs. I love where Christ has brought me. The journey with Him is full of small miracles, wisdom, His strength, and the opportunities He has given me to teach, to pray, to love, to serve.

Michele Dudas

In my busy and full life of "retirement" I felt called to work with women, to guide and teach them to deepen their walk with God. Although it has taken me many years to understand it, I know the Creator of the Universe is also my friend. I want to help others to see this in their lives through women's ministry and outreach in the community.

Several years ago I began to work part time as office manager at Christ for Life Sk8 Church, an indoor skate boarding facility that is, bottom line, a ministry. What an adventure it was for over four years! I didn't just organize and run the small office, I got to meet and know and hopefully influence the at-risk teens who we served. Sk8 Church remains one of my "families" with God at the center, and I am ever grateful and always amazed that God put me there at that particular point in my life.

I sometimes feel as if I'm not doing enough. Then I realize that I've always been that way—beating myself up for not being perfect enough, caring enough, sacrificing enough, smart enough. And part of my growing in God knows that all these things are whisperings of the enemy, of the self-doubt which, I believe, is Satan's greatest tool. I don't buy into it any more. I cannot do enough or be enough to make God love me more. When these ideas creep into my consciousness, I turn to God and ask His forgiveness and His power to resist. I know God loves me as I am and His love for me is boundless, unceasing, a forever thing.

Truthfully, God is what I am all about these days. He really is my #1. Since that's the truth for me, the rest of my relationships fall into place as I believe they should. I have a loving, supportive marriage, a peaceful family, good health and an energetic life, and many opportunities to serve my Lord and Savior. My faith and trust in Him is absolute. And, because I feel so blessed, my constant prayer is that should bad things happen, God will see me through just as He has through many ups and downs over the years, even before I knew His full power and love. One of my favorite verses in the Bible is Jeremiah 29:11 which says, *For I know the plans I have for you, declares the Lord, plans to prosper you and not to harm you, plans to give you a hope and a future.* I believe that those words spoken through the prophet Jeremiah so long ago apply to us today. God does have a plan for our lives if we will only open ourselves up to it and let Him in.

I am grateful for over seventy years of life, and I pray that however many more years I am allowed on this earth, I will use them to please Him. I pray, dear friend, that you too have found Him in your life and that your remaining years will be full of His amazing joy and contentment and peace.

Michele Dudas

Joyful in Him!
Michele

Trials Blessed by One Another

Denise Gardner

I have told you these things, so that in me you may have peace. In this world you will have trouble. But take heart! I have overcome the world. John 16:33

Adversity tinges life with a grey cloud of bleakness. My life was forecast to be mostly sunny. Storms were fleeting and did very little damage. I was not personally, intimately, or face-to-face familiar with worldly struggles like poverty, hunger, abuse, sickness, disease or death. I thought these kinds of sorrows belonged to other people, people in faraway places. Of course, I would see heart-breaking images on TV or read about devastating tragedies in newspapers. All of it tugged at my heart and made me sad, but I was so young and quite sheltered. The images were transitory and not very real or tangible. Most of my childhood days were filled with routine, chores, love, play, discipline and faith. My Roman Catholic upbringing threaded throughout my childhood like a tightly woven tapestry. I never strayed too far from the black and white, the here and now. A parochial picture depicted my family, my church, my school and my friends.

In my childhood, traditional holidays and holy days were more magical than spiritual. I did not know, therefore I could not understand, a need for salvation let alone a Savior. Fortunately, I grew up in a faith-based home that assured God is good and Baby Jesus is precious. The deeper issues of faith were not on my comprehension radar. Not yet anyway.

Of all the trimmings and trappings of the holidays (from Easter eggs to Christmas trees) the advent wreath has come to be the most symbolic of my life-long faith walk. Curious choice, considering many Christian denominations do not even use it during the Christmas season. However, our family's parish church always set up a big advent wreath near the altar. A beautiful decoration though I did not understand much of its symbolism. My memory of celebrating Jesus' birth with an advent wreath includes a large circle of evergreen boughs sprouting purple, pink and white candles emitting holy glowing flames. As a child I was wide-eyed and awe-filled by its superficial, beckoning beauty. I could not have known then the advent wreath would later tell the story of Jesus' role, as well as the body of Christ's, in my life trials. For me, the advent wreath is a personal, transcendent symbol bridging temporal trials to divine redemption.

I had an epiphany of Jesus working in my life and heart during my pivotal trial of breast cancer. During Christmas 2005, the advent wreath took on a whole new meaning filling me with a spiritual awakening and divine grace. My beloved husband calls this on-coming period of challenge "From Adversity to Advent." Each element of the wreath became part of my journey. I came to realize it is symbolic of every believer's journey through the highs and lows, the ups and downs, the ins and outs of this earthly life.

I am the light of the world. Whoever follows me will never walk in darkness, but will have the light of life. John 8:12

My own progression of faith as a believer mirrored the elements of the advent wreath. I am not a theologian or scholar of Christian symbolism. I can only share what was put in my distressed mind and laid upon my seeking heart as I traveled through a very dark and frightening health crisis.

The first purple candle, the Patriarch candle, I call my KNOWING Jesus candle. (*I will give them a heart to know me, that I am the Lord.*

Jeremiah 24:7) Like Abraham, Moses and Jacob of the Old Testament, I came to know God as the great I AM. In my mind, God was a huge "something." But, my small, hungry heart had not yet received Him. Like a sponge I had soaked up years of religious teachings about the elusive, unapproachable, all-powerful God of Creation, of wars and plagues, of arks and rainbows, of whales and lion dens, of miracles and mysteries, of thou shall and thou shall not. My Catholic education from kindergarten through college jam-packed my head with a concrete, intellectual image of God. But where could or would I find the heart and soul of my faith?

The second purple candle in the advent wreath is the Prophecy candle. This was my pathway to UNDERSTANDING Jesus. (...*to love Him with all your heart, with all your understanding and all your strength...* Mark 12:33) God through the Holy Spirit touched my heart and soul with a glimmer of hope, something more, something deeper and more meaningful than just studying books. The prophets of the Old Testament shared the hope of the promise of God sending a Savior. Isaiah and the other major and minor prophets eloquently and convincingly described the promise of salvation by a Messiah. (*But Israel will be saved by the Lord, with an everlasting salvation.* Isaiah 45:17) I came to understand the "way" to Jesus was more than simply knowledge or intellect. My cold, smart heart needed to be cracked and thawed so my soul could receive Him. There was a core element of divine passion stirred within me. In His perfect provision, God brought people into my life that love Jesus. I call these friends "beloved" even today. They are my brothers and sisters in Christ. I cherish each one of them for the seeds of love they have sowed in my heart and soul. My new other "family" is a crazy quilt of Christ followers who love me as Jesus loves me. At the time I did not realize the connection. Through them was forged a relationship with the risen Son of God. He lives in my wimpy, wishful heart. In the beginning I was confused, defensive and afraid. I just did not quite trust where loving Jesus was going to take me. I had been comfortable in my academic box of facts and logic. Now God was taking the lid off that trap to infuse love, hope and truth into every molecule of my DNA, the very substance He Himself created as me.

The only pink candle, the Shepherd's candle, reflects my season of SEEKING Jesus. (*But seek first His kingdom and His righteousness, and all these things will be given to you as well.* Matthew 6:33) My new, God given friends, my family in Christ, invited me into a way of living where Jesus is very real, all the time. Jesus is everything. I want to know, really know Jesus. I have humbled myself to try to understand Him, although much of faith often remains a mystery. I seek to be a disciple, which requires discipling. I actively try to look for Jesus everywhere and in everyone. I repeatedly discover Him truly everywhere and to be in everyone even when it may not seem so obvious.

The shepherds were not intellectuals. They found Jesus in a lowly manger after seeking Him because of an angel's message. (*...and the sheep listen to His voice. He calls His own sheep by name and leads them out.* John 10:4) The shepherds were actually there in real time. Being present opened up their minds and hearts to know here was their long awaited Savior. I desperately wanted this kind of awakening. I dug into the Word with insatiable hunger by joining my first Bible study. I have since been a part of so many wonderful, diverse groups of seekers and believers also hungry for Jesus. Whenever I can, I listen to Christian music, Christian talk radio and Christian sermons on podcasts. Being "filled-up" feels good, very good.

Like many activities or interests a detrimental, obsession can creep in and take over the pursuit. In my seeking I was so busy, I was wearing myself out. While I was trying so hard to find Him, I failed to notice He was right with me, everywhere, all the time. I knew I needed to slow down or I would burn out. A quiet pursuit of just being in His presence was what I needed. The joy of Jesus is in being with Him, talking to Him and listening for Him.

Stress, over commitment, and exhaustion were manifested in my diagnosis of breast cancer. God did not cause me to get cancer, but I think He allowed me to experience it. The diagnosis slowed me down. Lying in bed after chemotherapy treatments and surgery forced me into a quiet time I am not sure I would have found otherwise. In this space I found a divine joy that had little to do with the circumstances of my life (breast cancer) and had a lot to do with the state of my aching heart. This transformed my relationship with Jesus to one with less rigidity and ritual and more acceptance and peace. God has brought me to a place where my faith is stronger and my relationship with Him is more real and intimate. I am capable of bearing more of life challenges because my trust lies in Jesus alone. What trials I had been through with breast cancer and those on my horizon were testimonies to the body of Christ, those who believe in Him. I saw how I am part of God's plan. His perfect will pushed me where I never imagined I would go.

The third purple candle is the Angel candle representing the divine spark, the holy flash of my FINDING Jesus and humbly claiming Him my Lord, Master and Savior. (*Ask and it will be given to you; seek and you will find; knock and the door will be open to you. For everyone who asks receives; he who seeks finds; and to him who knocks, the door will be opened.* Matthew 7:7-8) Through the uninvited adversity and monumental challenges of breast cancer, I ultimately found Jesus. Sweeping moments of fear, anger, denial, guilt, bargaining and self-pity all became part of finding Him and facing Him. I desperately wanted to leave the low, sinking place I had found myself in and move to more hopeful, higher ground. I discovered His absolute, unconditional, never failing and perfect love for me. I sought, asked and invited Him into my heart and my life, messy as it was and still is. I surrendered to Him daily as I was catapulted into the unknown and frightening medical territory of poking, prodding, tests, blood draws, biopsies, surgery, chemotherapy and reconstruction.

The body is a unit, though it is made up of many parts, and though the parts are many, they form one body. So it is with Christ. 1Corinthians 12:12-13

I became the "receiver" of the immeasurable kindness of others, from my husband, my sons, my sisters, old friends and new—even strangers. This was not a comfortable role to assume, but it was the only part I could play. I was scared, I was sick and I was tired. My lack of energy reminded me to surrender. I also became an observer. I was part of the believers God created to be the "Body of Christ." Jesus is the "Head" and His church (His followers) are the eyes, the ears, the mouth, the hands, the feet and the backbone all meant to participate in God's perfect plan and purpose for this world. This is so all people come to know Jesus and thereby come into relationship with God just as He intended from His first breath of creation.

In the posture of surrender, rendered by breast cancer, I was witness to the body of Christ in full action. In my slow state of being I watched how generously people loved me and loved one another. I call this activity of the body of Christ "one anothering." In this "one anothering" I found Jesus. And I made the passage into knowing what I know as Truth. In my struggles and through others' acts of service I proclaimed the Name of Jesus as Truth! I was no longer reluctant, afraid or ashamed. Imagine! All of this personal, glorious epiphany sprouted from destructive, marauding cancer cells! I received a peace and assurance that if I would die from breast cancer, I was now fully living in the grace and love of Jesus. God knew exactly what He was doing when He allowed cancer into my life. I learned to trust Him in this trial and all those to come. I am glad I did and I am humbly grateful.

Some advent wreaths have a fifth white candle in the center of the other four. I choose to include this Christ candle in my wreath as a symbol of transcendence. I cannot help but want to SHARE Jesus' love with others. Jesus is at the center of my life.

He is The *Way, the Truth and the Life.* John 14:6

He is the eternal *Light of the world.* John 8:12

I have learned, and experienced, out of adversity will come an advent, a coming of sorts.....a coming to Jesus. In Jesus coming to us, being born in a lowly manger we witness the "one anothering" of the patriarchs, the prophets, the angels, the shepherds and all believers through all of time. Our time on earth is tough and tangled, but He has come! Jesus lives!

My devoted, faithful, tenacious and loving husband championed my breast cancer challenge. God put us together long ago knowing we would have great shared joys but also together face many crises. Needless to say, breast cancer was a biggie. My husband "one anothered" me and allowed others to use their gifts in "one anothering" us. My husband acted on absolute faith and trust in Jesus who would lead the way. God was with us every step of the way. He always provides. He is forever faithful. I am grateful my husband travels the faith journey with me. I will never undervalue this blessing.

My fervent prayer is for everyone to realize his or her need for Jesus. I long for each tender, broken heart to answer His knock and let Him in. Let others in, too! I sound the divine trumpet call for "one anothering" in the face of your, or someone else's, trials. There is holy transcendence in surrendering to Jesus and embracing the body of Christ. Begin to "one another" and experience the fullness of His perfect grace.

God's Word tells us:
Pray for one another. James 5:16
Encourage one another. Hebrews 3:13
Build one another up. 1Thessalonians 5:11
Bear one another's burdens. Galatians 6:2
Love one another. John 13:34-35
Be devoted to one another. Romans 12:10
Serve one another. Galatians 5:13
Submit to one another. Ephesians 5:21
Spur one another on. Hebrews 10:24
Be hospitable to one another. 1Peter 4:8-9
Greet one another. Romans 16:16

Storms gather. Grey clouds loom. Life often looks bleak, but in all the darkness is a light. Choose to seek and follow the Light, Jesus. We are all wounded. We all face trials. We will again and again, this side of Heaven. Each of us is blessedly gifted to "one another" each other in this broken, messy, crazy, beautiful world. We are called to be healers in whatever capacity. Will you surrender your wounds to the transcending power of Christ in every and all things? Will you do it as part of the body of Christ, broken as each of us is, for one another? Bring your faith and your life full circle into the transcendent message of the advent wreath where you come to KNOW, UNDERSTAND, SEEK, FIND and SHARE Jesus with one another.

Denise Gardner
and certified therapy dog Willie

The Greater the Reward – the Greater the Test
The Greater the Victory – the Greater the Battle

Jade Getchell

And greater that battle it has been… I do not have all the answers. I probably do not even have some of them. What I do have is my own battle with a testimony of how I overcame those battles through the power of Jesus, the presence of the Holy Spirit, and protection of God on me every day of my life. Sort of the like the addict who has used heroine for years and looks back questioning how they made it out alive, I am amazed at God's perfect love and grace who kept me wrapped in His arms and safe from harm.

There have always been pieces of me that never felt good enough. Moments of staring at myself in a mirror, criticizing my body, and shaming myself are all memories from my not-so-distant past. My relationship with a mirror is similar to that of an abusive relationship. I know it is not good for me and yet I keep going back, time and time again. It hurts, and digs, and burns, and pierces to the center of my core… but I keep going back. In being completely transparent, I have never been happy with myself until now, seventeen years later.

The first time I can remember observing my body and weight was in high school, at fifteen years old and on hundred twenty pounds. I attended a performing arts high school where you had to fit (for the most part) in pre-made costumes. The costume room was overwhelming for someone like me. As I walked in the door, one large room filled with aisles of costumes repeated themselves. Feathers, sequins, suits, headdresses, and bodysuits, surrounded me. Each aisle was two or three racks high floor to ceiling. Seeing breathtaking costumes I could not fit into was a heart wrenching feeling. All of the other girls could wear them because they were thin, beautiful, drop-dead knockouts. Perfectly shaped, proportioned, and solid muscle. I felt I was the ugly duckling of the group. I can recall a time when my bust had to be duct taped – literally duct taped – to fit in the costume so it could be zipped up. Humiliating is the only term to describe this experience. (For a good laugh, imagine how it felt taking the duct tape OFF!)

I lost ten pounds in my junior year in high school. I remember standing in front of a dance mirror in a pair of black fitted pants with a tank top, v-neck shirt with black, green, and white horizontal stripes that stopped right at my hip area. As I stood in front of this mirror, I looked my body over trying desperately to figure out what had changed that everyone continuously complimented me on. The feeling of acceptance and affirmation was what I had longed for.

After graduating high school, I never really paid attention to my body anymore. I ran away, got married and gained twenty pounds weighing in at one hundred thirty five pounds. During the time I was married (which no one knew about), I began to realize my actions of running away and getting married were all in rebellion to God. I struggled with thoughts that I had failed God. He must be so angry at me. After all, I had been disobedient in so many areas (which allowed for the mess I was in). Growing up, disappointment from my parents was far worse than any spanking. Thinking I had disappointed God was something I did not know how to process.

I began to pray to God an overly-simple prayer, "If I have made a mistake God, please allow him to ask for a divorce so I may remarry according to your Word. If I have not, please help us to work things out."

God answered my prayer. Six months later, my husband asked me for a divorce. God had shown up for little-ole-me, the girl who acted foolish and rebellious not only to Him but to my parents. By nineteen years old, I was going through the divorce process (which no one knew about).

He showed up for me in the first serious prayer I can ever remember praying. I had gained my first step of faith in trusting God. This newfound faith gave me courage to come clean with my parents about what I had done and where I was in the process of trying to correct it. God's Word says truth will set us free... being honest with my parents lifted a weight from my shoulders that is indescribable.

In August of 2002, my divorce was final. It was time to make myself over both physically and mentally. As a woman, sometimes a makeover is all we need to feel better! For the physical portion of the makeover, I colored my hair, chopped it off, and began exercising. I developed a regiment of 3-4 days a week of 30-45 minutes on a treadmill. I loved the euphoric high of accomplishment and endorphins rushing throughout my mind. Essentially, you feel a healthy competition with yourself.

For the mental portion of the makeover, I vowed to not date for a year to discover who I was again and to focus on God. With my newfound faith, I was ready to discover more about God. What was He like? What did He think of me? I wanted to learn more about Him because He was my new relationship. Having returned to the church I attended before I ran away and got married, I also returned to the worship team. On a Sunday morning (December 14, 2003) I walked into rehearsal and saw a guy standing on stage playing the bass. He was broad shouldered, dressed in baggy jeans, a light blue Aeropostale hoodie, and beanie. The hood of the hoodie was pulled up. When I discovered who it was I was floored. His name was Shane. We had known each other for years, but he was younger than me so I never paid much attention through our teenage years. He used to be scrawny from what I could remember – boy did he grow up! I asked him to a movie that night and a week later we were officially dating. He was fabulously sexy, sweet, talented, popular and had the cool car. Everything you could ask for. To this day, I can remember the butterflies I had on our first date. After seeing the movie, we were playing pool and he leaned in and kissed me. Oh! I remember thinking to myself, *Did he really just kiss me?!* I was smitten!

With a new man in my life and still exercising, I did not realize I was eating only a piece of toast a day and drinking coffee. Down from a size five and medium or large shirts, I was wearing size one jeans and small shirts. "I must be doing something right!" I thought to myself. I loved the way I felt. I loved hearing others tell me how good I looked. *Who does not like to hear how good they look?* Everyone enjoys hearing positive reinforcement. I was soaking up what others were saying because I was empty in so many other areas.

The words other people speak can be deceiving. It's so important to have a solid relationship with God so He can prick your heart when something isn't right. My relationship with God now, at thirty-three years old, is much more mature than where it was at twenty-one years old. As we grow in Him and with Him, clearly hearing from God becomes easier and easier. God is such a sweet God to me, He will prick my heart if I begin to get on a self-destructive track again. He loves me so much He will do whatever it takes to get my attention.

After eight or nine months, I surpassed the "looking good" point. My cheekbones had sunken, my collarbones were sticking out, my skin was nauseatingly pale, and I was losing my hair. As I shampooed my hair, clumps of hair came out in my hands. I would sit on my shower floor sobbing, hair in hand. I had bald spots on my scalp where no hair existed anymore. I had no definition or shape to me, only skin that hung without elasticity. Tears came so hard that my eyes were physically in pain.

When it is YOU filling yourself up, YOU cannot sustain it the right way. I was so, so empty in so many ways and yet I had no idea how to fill the voids I felt. I chased what I thought would fill me up. Boys had not filled my void, fitness had not filled my void. My void still existed. Looking back, I realized I chased what I could control. I chose what to eat, I chose how much to exercise. I... I... I... Do you see a pattern? Even with my new relationship with God, I still had a very selfish heart. My eyes were on myself and not Him. It's possible to have a relationship with God but not know Him at all.

Jade Getchell

I can remember the day I finally admitted to myself I had an eating disorder. No one wants to admit they have a problem. But I knew the first step towards correcting my problem was to admit it to myself and to someone else. I called my sister and brother-in-law and met them in a Wendy's parking lot at Mars Hill Road and Dallas Hwy. My heart was jumping out of my chest. I could hear every heart beat and my palms were sweating, as I looked them in the eyes. The words struggled to come out of my mouth. Each time I would try to speak, I would choke up. I tried again. As tears swelled up and then spilled down my cheeks, I said it.

"I have a problem."

It was simplest of sentences but one with a huge release of freedom.

Jesus, yet again, showed up for me. He had brought me to the realization that I had a problem and gave me the courage and strength to speak it out loud. He was with me every step of the way.

In a time where I felt I was losing control, the very thing I had fought so hard to have and keep, my family was there supporting me. They may not have been able to understand what I was going through, or why I was going through it, but they were still supportive and that meant the world to me. Physically, my eating disorder was never severe enough to be hospitalized for treatment. Mentally, it was the greatest struggle I had faced in my life. If I were an alcoholic, I would need to stay away from beer and liquor. If I were a drug addict, I would need to stay away from illegal drugs and prescription pills. When the problem is you, how do you stay away from yourself? The process of saving me from myself is my testimony. It's a process, much like anything God tries to teach us, of learning, trying, and failing, then trying again.

I began eating again and WHOA did I suffer consequences from this. The weight came back – in a double portion – and I do not mean in the "anointing" kind of way. I tried to maintain my weight through exercise. What began as three to four days a week of 30-45 minutes each day turned into five days a week, at least 1–1.5 hours at the gym. I would run, twisting my core back and forth violently, until my midsection hurt. My thighs felt like Jello from running faster than my feet could keep up. My legs would be so unstable the muscle fibers continued twitching for another five minutes, not allowing me to walk easily. Maintaining my weight became such a priority for me, my gym time came at the expense of friends, family, my boyfriend, and life events. All that mattered to me was completing my work out for the day. My life was completely unbalanced and upside down in priorities. The need to control my weight was overtaking my life. I was no longer obsessed with food; I was obsessed with the treadmill and how my body felt even if I was killing it. I substituted one issue for another.

In the name of control, I was punishing myself for eating. If I ate fast food, I felt I had to work out again. If I ate cake, I had to do an extra twenty minutes of running. If I ate cookies, I needed to do some extra ab and core work. The process was mentally devastating and physically exhausting. There were times my head was spinning out of control without the ability to stop. I could not gain control. Again, substituting one thing for another.

What I never anticipated in all of this was the side effects of starvation, over exercising, and the human body. While Jesus did help me along the way by reminding me I had the courage to face these hardships in my life, I still had the consequences of my decisions. Do not misunderstand my words here; Jesus and God are as big as it gets and they can do whatever they choose to, including allowing someone to not have to suffer consequences of their decisions. In my personal experience however, we learn from our mistakes and God knows this since He created us. Like a good father, our Father allowed me to experience the consequences of my actions. This made me stronger. If a thought creeps back into my mind about controlling food or exercising, I immediately think of the consequences. It's enough to remind me I do not need to go down this road again.

Looking back, no matter how hard I tried, I could never fill the void inside of me. This feeling of not being accepted, not being loved, and not reaching a certain standard plagued me. Everything I did was in vain. I hurt family, friends, and I was killing myself (figuratively and literally) even though I could not see it. Most of all, I didn't love myself. Being 100% transparent, I hated myself and I was disgusted with myself. The saddest part is I cannot pinpoint what exactly I hated so badly. Food is not my enemy and neither is exercise. I did not realize moderation is how you manage these things. Moderation is key to a healthy lifestyle with food and fitness.

Fast-forward a year. My sister and I began going to fitness classes together at a local gym. Working out with her was one of the best things I have ever done. She became my accountability partner by being painfully honest in the areas I needed to hear it most. Yet, she still pushed me in the areas I could handle. God knew she was the perfect fit for me at this time in my life. We went to group fitness classes four times a week for an hour. This time it was different. Each class was different: a martial arts class, a light weights class for toning, a hip-hop dance class, and a high intensity cardio class. They were so much fun! I didn't realize you could actually enjoy working out! I enjoyed what we did together and I ate what I wanted within reason. For the first time in my life I could eat a piece of pizza without shame. For the first time, for as far back as I can remember, I accepted my own body. I had finally found balance and moderation. Instead of looking at myself critically in the mirror, I was looking at the positive changes coming through.

In April of 2009, Shane proposed to me and in September of the same year we were married. If I can toot my own horn, in my wedding gown, I looked the best I had ever looked. As random as this sounds, for the first time I did not have a single thought of "how does my body look" on that day or on my honeymoon. I was beyond confident in my skin for the first time in my life.

God had sent me someone who was divinely set aside for me. God wasn't mad at me for my former mistakes; but instead, forgave me for them and blessed me with a lifelong husband. The right husband. There is no better feeling than knowing you are with the one person God set aside for you—and you only find this person when you are living in His righteousness. Shane is an exceptional man. He is a man I am proud to say I am married to.

I had a great life. Even though God had blessed me with a new husband, my dream SUV, an amazing first home in the country on an acre of land, a job I never had to get dressed up to go to, and a new home church, something was missing. All of this filled my life, the "things" we desire in life, and yet, something was still missing. Eventually, the insecurities of my body began to creep back. Before I knew it, I was back to looking in the mirror. This time was slightly different. (The devil is smart enough to change his tactics just a smidge.)

The mirror shows us a reflection of what is actually there. No tricks, only truth. Whether we choose to accept what we see is up to us, for the good and for the bad. A mirror does not play tricks, but our mind can. My mind was showing me all the things my body "didn't have." It would exaggerate body parts as if I were standing in front of a carnival mirror. Instead of seeing abs beginning to show through, all I could see was a rear end two times the size it should be. I saw droopy arms and thighs that jiggled. Flabbiness, flabbiness everywhere! Piece by piece I picked my body apart until there was nothing left to choose.

The cycle had begun again. Mental games and manipulation from my own mind, but it was much stronger this time. I struggled internally for years. No one knew. It was a private game between me, myself, and I. I am sure certain family members had suspicions of "something"' going on but could not put their finger on what it could be. I had become professional at plastering on the "everything is great" face disguising my real pain. I could mask everything with the best of them but deep inside was screaming out for someone to understand what was happening. I made a comment once to a friend of how "I don't want to be rid of the fear of how I look. If I do, then I may not care, and it could all go the opposite way." Sad, huh? My mind was so wrapped around this ideological concept, I was sincerely lost. I would later learn I was suffering from was called Battle Dysmorphia.

As a child, I knew God existed and that He was there to answer my prayers. I knew of the Holy Spirit but only as a character in the Bible. In 2010, I discovered the gifts of the Spirit were alive and living.

I was waiting in the sanctuary for drama team practice to begin, and thirty minutes later my sister pulled me into "the loft" (the youth room). When I walked in, the kids I had been waiting for in the sanctuary were praying, dancing, shouting, and surrendering their all to God. They were leaving nothing back in worshipping God. (If we would stop long enough to watch those younger than us we might just learn something!

Jade Getchell

We can learn something from anyone. Age is just a number.) I was in a horrible mood as it was, and I didn't want to be there. I took a seat in an empty chair, leaned forward, placed my forearms on my knees, and closed my eyes. Slowly, I felt my body begin to get warm. My heart began pounding in my chest. I began praying simple sentences to God, nothing ornate. A strong desire to feel what those kids were feeling swelled inside of me. I now know what they were feeling—it was the Holy Spirit taking hold of me. My stomach burned and I had a level of uneasiness in me that was indescribable. If I could have screamed in that moment, maybe I could have relieved the pressure building up inside of me. Before I knew it, I was doubled over on the floor crying. I do not mean subtle, tears streaming down my face, one tear at a time sort of cry. I mean the full-on snot-out- the-nose on the carpet, gasping for air, sounding like a madwoman cry. (Don't try for a second to tell yourself you do not know what I am talking about! Every woman has had a snot cry!) One young lady reached down and touched my stomach and began praying for me. She was saying things in her prayer no one else knew about! She was praying for me to be delivered of this wretched issue and move on. I knelt where I was stunned, staring at her. How did she know? How did this eighteen-year-old girl know what I was doing in the dark? I'll tell you how... the Lord.

Luke 8:17, *For there is nothing hidden that will not be disclosed, and nothing concealed that will not be known or brought out into the open.*

Mark 4:22, *For everything that is hidden will eventually be brought into the open, and every secret will be brought to light.*

I fell to the floor, shouting the words, "I don't want this anymore! I don't want this anymore!" Before I knew it I had shouted, "I don't want this eating disorder anymore!" It was over. The building pressure in my stomach was gone. My anxiety, gone. I went home and ate a doughnut for the first time without remorse. God had delivered me from my issue once and for all! To this day, I cannot explain how I know this, but this time was different. I had never encountered God the way I did that day.

Today, I see that being so focused on my weight, or my image means meant I was not focused enough on God. If I have time to dwell and worry about something, then I am not spending enough time focusing on God. Every day is a choice to make the right decisions. A decision to choose to eat and not over-exercise, a decision to accept myself for who I was created to be, a decision to make me the best me I can be, are all decisions I have made.

I am one choice away from being back where I was. Every day is <u>another</u> day I have the opportunity to thank God for hand picking me for Himself, carrying me in my moments of destruction, and never giving up on me. He is still choosing to bless me! After seven years of destruction to my body—He gave me a new mindset to appreciate who God created me to be.

On August 17, 2011, I found out I was pregnant. This was a gift from God I never would have been able to receive had I continued a destructive path on destroying my body. How's that for miracles?! Elijah went to be with Jesus ten weeks later. I had a strange miscarriage, which I wrote about in numerous posts in my blog. On December 24, 2011, I found out I was pregnant again with our daughter. She is everything we asked for and more. God answered every prayer we prayed over her, down to eye color. I added to the prayers for God to allow me to experience a pain free birth. He answered! I have no idea what a contraction feels like. I like favor!

I share my testimony with you because the Bible states, "... *always be prepared to make a defense to anyone who asks you for a reason for the hope that is in you* (1 Peter 3:15). Hope is defined as a feeling of expectation and desire for a certain thing to happen.

With God, we mix hope, faith, and prayer to trust for the most favorable outcome possible that is good for us. How often we desire something in life, but God knows it's not the best for us. My story continues to grow. Every day, month, and year adds to this chapter. I encourage you to keep reading my story at www.confessionletters.com.

We can be a person of great faith or a person of great doubt. Room does not exist for both. If we allow ourselves to be overcome with the things our flesh takes us through, we will end up miserable. I know this all too well. My emotional roller coaster was a ride I never intended on riding to begin with, and one I never intend on riding again. Do we ever actually intend on these things? These moments are important to go though. You cannot grow without growing pains. You cannot help others find their way through trials if you have never found your way through them. Our faith cannot expand unless we have times of being uncomfortable, not understanding, and frustration. How can you truly appreciate what victory is if you have never experienced failure?

I don't have all the answers. I probably don't even have some of them. What I do have is my own experiences and how they have influenced my life. I am created with an ability to view things differently than others. Many think I always try to purposely view something opposite of them, but I do not. It is just how I am wired. This is my same ability with faith. We are told time and time again, "Just have faith. Have faith and everything will work out!" They make it sound like this amazing thing (which it is) is super easy to do. I am here to tell you, it's okay to feel like it is uncomfortable and scary.

Walking in faith doesn't always look pretty and it hardly ever feels pretty. My story ends with favor. Favor is not always comfortable. Do you think Mary was comfortable with the favor of carrying Jesus? I think not. Generally speaking, faith is anything but comfortable. The deeper I go with God in my walk of faith, the harder it becomes; however, the greater the experience is with God in the end. For me, there is no turning back. Each experience with God simply makes me yearn for the next.

Jade Getchell

Photography by: Camille Youngblood Photography
www.facebook.com/Camilleyoungbloodphotography

Dangerous Times and Oblivious Parenting— My Love Affair with the Bondage Breaker

Susan Hamilton

No, I did NOT enjoy parenting. It sucked. I really thought I was good at it, but alas, I was a horrible mother. I prayed about it constantly, but my kids really hated me. Still do, if you want to know the truth about it. This is absolutely the generation Paul warned Timothy about, and I was completely unprepared.

My oldest son started experiencing trouble when we lost our country home and had to move into the "burbs." A couple of years prior to that, we had skyrocketed to a six-figure income and moved our five children to an acre just outside of town. Our jet-set lifestyle easily accepted cocaine, as long as the kids couldn't see it. Of course, we never thought they saw anything. Cocaine allowed us to be super-human, drinking absurd amounts of alcohol with our childless neighbors and still able to function—though barely—the next day.

Then the Twin Towers went down, and my husband's ability to run communication for his new startup company came to a grinding halt, so did investor interest. And we were high.

Drugs are so terribly deceitful. Don't ever let anyone tell you they make you feel awful, because that's exactly where we lose our clout with our kids. All they see is the hype and the fun, and if you don't admit it, you'll lose face fast. Yeah, they're fun alright. But I promise you, that first experience, if it doesn't kill you, will absolutely lie to you. If you don't find a new crowd quick, you'll chase that first high for years and never reach it again. Eventually, *you do feel awful*. And you spend all your money and time trying to find the drug that never quite feels as good as it did the first time you used it. When you're in the zone, operating between highs and lows, you never even see what you're doing to your life. Meanwhile, you turn on each other and nearly kill each other. At least ... that's what we did.

We refused to look at our finances until our boat was repossessed. Then they took the truck, and foreclosed on our house. We had no credit, no money, no work—and I remember the principals at the elementary, middle and high school helped us feed the kids out of their own pockets until we qualified for government assistance. The vehicle we had left had no seat belts, was out of inspection and registration, and since no one would rent us a home with such crappy credit, I was fairly certain we would end up sleeping in that old suburban under an overpass, only to have our kids taken from us. Since this experience, believe it or not at your own peril, **I've seen much worse destruction.** The hand of God was upon us, even then.

My mother eventually allowed me to work as a receptionist for their company. The office was only a couple miles down the road, and I could walk there. I started making some money, but when everything you do is so difficult and all you're focused on is how much you want to feel better than you do, it's not hard to talk yourself into spending "just a little'" on some junk to pass the time. Oops, there went the check. I did that for about a month. My husband and I were violently angry with each other all the time. At least when we were high we would have sex. No intimacy, just a Band-Aid to cover a disdain for one another that became apparent to everyone around us. Including the kids. Cocaine makes you feel like you can do everything you need to do, only better. I could keep an amazingly clean home, make great dinners out of nothing and never feel drunk. I always wondered, *Who wouldn't want to feel like this?* We had slowed way down, but wouldn't turn down a 'bump.' That would just be stupid.

We continued to look for another home to rent within the next 30 days so we could get the $300 the bank was willing to give us just to leave our country home. One day, I was working in the office with my sister and left to go grab some burgers. When I got back, she was smiling. One of the people I had spoken with about a rental and had previously turned me down, called to check my references again. She got my sister. They got into some weird conversation, "Was I clean? Would I take care of the house? What were my kids like?" This woman had been through hell with her last tenants, and after speaking with my sister, was willing to give us a try!

$300, a paid for vehicle, a place to live, and a job. Bread crumbs of Jesus.

As we packed up our lost dream home, I noticed my second grader's drawings in the rec room. Stick figures with clouds over their heads and exclamation points, with angry expressions and some words he could spell. Page after page. This is where we thought the kids were "not noticing" our behavior.

We moved into the teeny-tiny home so grateful. Somehow, we crammed thirty-eight hundred square feet of stuff into eighteen hundred square feet of space.

We were far away from anyone who was using, and it looked like we were going to make it after all. I had begun tithing my little check, but I didn't tell my husband. See, for the last year, I had handled my hangovers in bed watching Joyce Meyer on TBN. He already thought I was nuts. I was a Christian for the first twenty minutes of my day, and a demon for the rest of it. He wasn't much better, but had even less interest in that faith garbage.

Randy began working for a furniture company making deliveries with the truck and trailer. He was paid well, and often tipped. It was hard work. He carried mattresses on his back up flights of stairs for hours, day after day. He never turned down a job. I continued to work for my parents' company. As soon as we paid our bills, I went to the grocery store. There was nothing left in our account when I was done, but we were recovering. It felt good. We ate beans and rice, quesadillas, soups and pancakes. I could really stretch a dollar! (Crazy, this is one of the kids' favorite memories.)

Still, through it all, we never said we'd avoid our old relationships. We never said we'd completely stop using. We just thought we ought to calm down. Pretty soon, old friends started coming around to see how we were doing. We had no conviction about what it would truly take to change our lives.

After a few drinks we'd start asking each other if we wanted to go in on a drug purchase. An eight ball would keep a party of six people drinking and talking all night. The kids would go to sleep and none would be the wiser. The next day, we'd be exhausted and unable to communicate. I would lose my voice, Randy would lose his hearing, and we'd be thoroughly disgusted with each other for days. We started having to tell our debtors that we'd have to make payment arrangements.

One day, **we absolutely decided to stop using**. We were sick of fighting, and sick of the pain it was causing the kids. We were sick of being sick. Enough drugs. I couldn't talk him into going to church, but we both agreed the drugs had to go.

Sure enough, another weekend came around and another opportunity to use when friends showed up. We played cards, drank Southern Comfort and used cocaine all night. Normally, we would leave a couple of lines on the mirror for "breakfast" so we could manage the kids in the morning. This time, we woke up to nothing left. We were furious with each other for using the last of it only to go to sleep! We had done waaay too much cocaine.

I got up to take a shower. As I closed my eyes and leaned back into the shower, I realized the tiles were moving. I was seeing dragons. They were cartoonish, but so real. They were in my head. I opened my eyes and they were still there. I could not get those dragons to go away, knowing they weren't there, but seeing them clearly. I thought, *Oh, no, I can't control my thoughts!* And then I thought, *No. Jesus, save me now. I've been a fool! Take my brain, don't let me lose my mind.* I kept thinking about what my kids would see if I died at that moment. I realized they would go through my things and know I was really, really, horrible. I realized they would feel betrayed and damaged, and it hurt so bad. My head was spinning. *Take over now, Jesus, PLEASE!!* And then out loud I said, "I give You control, please take it."

I went back to bed and just laid there. The dragons had stopped. It was over, and I was numb all over my body and mind. A couple days later I called my big sister in Wisconsin and told her what I had done. To everyone's surprise, Randy agreed to let me stay with her for the weekend, and between them, they came up with the money for my plane ticket. I was baptized by her son in her bathtub that Sunday before I flew home the same night.

But we had surrounded ourselves with friendships that included drugs and children. To sever those relationships meant we had to sever our children's relationships, too. It was time. We had begun to see that the homes we were allowing our children to go to were degraded to unacceptable. This was getting really dangerous. They hated us for that.

I'll never forget the following two months. We had mood swings. We had arguments and health issues. We worked it all out, and started to see a better way to raise our family. Then one night at ten o'clock, the doorbell rang. We knew only certain people would come around at ten. Funny how when we were using a lot, we spent all our time looking for drugs, but after we actually decided to stop, drugs walked right up to our doorstep. Free. This is when I finally realized that drugs were a tool of the devil, and we had been happily letting him destroy us.

Randy answered the door. I was standing right beside him, with the door mostly closed. We wanted to have a united front. We were determined NOT to use. These friends hadn't been to our new location yet, and they were surprised and disappointed that we didn't let them come in.

When we closed the door and turned to go back to bed, we saw all our kids lined up on the stairwell, watching us. It was a pivotal moment. A conviction in my spirit. We looked at each other, knowingly, and ushered the kids to bed. We felt like we had passed a test.

It took two years to stop experiencing withdrawal symptoms. I was the slow lady on the highway, unable to drive past forty mph without extreme anxiety that included sweating, heart racing and the very real fear that I would black out at any second. I was easily depressed. Easily angry. But I knew that if I went to a doctor with these symptoms, they would put me on a medication that I would have to be weaned off, and I didn't want to exchange one addiction for another. I chose to run and lift weights, reasoning that I could sweat myself clean. The side effect was amazing; I was able to regulate the hormones I had screwed up for so long.

One day during my dry-out period, as I was putting clothes away, I opened my fifteen-year-old's top drawer. What on earth did anyone need fifteen lighters for? It hit me like a brick between my eyes. I had always figured if my kids ever played with drugs, they would begin with pot, as I had at fifteen. I was now strong enough and aware that if they ever did, I would be able to stop it in its tracks. Surely that's what God let me experience this for. But that was a big lie. Kids today don't start on pot. Whatever he was doing, he needed several lighters.

I immediately went to prayer. *What do I do? How do I stop this?* I had ignored letters from the school the past year, assuming they were just some sort of over-reporting, my kids NEVER had a bad report. No, he had skipped a LOT of school. Our son was in trouble. The Good Lord had pulled my head out of my butt in time to see what was happening to my family.

That was fifteen years ago. When I saw my son in trouble, I started hittin' the Book. I started looking for answers and spent hours on my knees and on my living room sofa private church. It wasn't the end of the destruction, it was only the beginning. Four of my five kids would eventually do time, some serious, some drug or alcohol induced stupid.

One of the ways I recovered physically was to work out hard, but I know now a renewed mind will heal a brain. I knew I could sweat out my toxins, and the added benefit was I accidentally solved what I learned later to be my jacked up hormone issues—all due to thinking I could experience my emotions on drugs. People say drugs are witchcraft. I don't. I know that in my case, I used drugs to manipulate everything I was going through. If I was happy, it was time to celebrate. If I was depressed, it was time to get high. If I was angry, we could get along if I was a little more numb. I could make myself get up and make myself go to sleep at will—all with drugs.

I remember the first time something wonderful happened to one of my kids and I had been drug free for a couple of months. I had absolutely no reaction. I wanted to react, but was incapable of a natural feeling. It was a very rude awakening, and it taught me so much. I wasn't guilty of witchcraft, I was guilty of idolatry. I gave something else preeminence only God had a right to have. Now I know I can experience my emotional life **with** my Father, and I'm so filled with His presence, peace and joy. Those words actually MEAN something. I value them highly. I value HIM highly.

It took a long time to heal, and during that time, I didn't have what some would call spiritual "success." It literally felt like someone was standing in front of me shooting machine gun bullets at me over and over and over again. My kids were REALLY struggling, and VERY hateful. *Why wouldn't God just STOP this??? Why was I still going through this same kind of pain, this same violent disrespect? This same argument with my husband? WHY wasn't it just going away, if I was so blessed?* I CLUNG to the Words and precepts I was learning, needing Jesus every breath.

Thing is, I didn't get in that mess overnight. I had deeply rooted issues that took a lot of deep, deep therapy —therapy only Jesus Himself could possibly provide. I knew I had failed at the only thing God had given me to do. I cried to Him regularly. I asked Him for a chance to correct it, for a "do-over." I don't advise that.

My adult, homeless, disrespectful children moved back in over ten times—always long enough for me to think I could help them with my better example, and always long enough to hurt me terribly. They didn't respect me. They didn't respect themselves. We learned at one point my youngest daughter, at nineteen, was stripping. Randy and I were determined to find her and rip her right off that pole. We prayed constantly for our children, and one day, she showed up on my doorstep.

She was overly made up, dressed provocatively, and where she got those boobs I had no idea. I slowly opened the back door and ushered her to the nearby kitchen table. I was not about to let her live with us again; she had told everyone that the reason she was homeless was because Randy beat her. She was crying, and lying, and I just sat there, trying not to be a cold b****. I knew God had brought her back to me, but had no idea what to do and how to love her. I was empty.

I left her at the table to take a shower and gather myself. I closed the door and dropped to my knees. "Father, what do you want me to do? How do I walk in love? She's your daughter, not mine. I don't know how to love her. I don't know how to not enable her. I feel nothing inside, forgive me, how do I show her compassion I don't have?"

So clearly He said to me, "Susan, remember how you thought I let you go through those things so you could keep your kids out of trouble? You were NEVER going to keep them from trouble, Susan, you couldn't have done that. But now, knowing what you know, you are the only one uniquely qualified to help her back up."

My heart changed in an instant. I couldn't wait to get downstairs and hold her. I cried for all she had lost. We hadn't hugged in years, she didn't expect it, and quite frankly, I thought she would pull away like she always did. This time, she melted into me. She needed me to love her, to accept her, and to help her. She needed her mother, and without the love of God in me, I would have been unable to give it to her. We cried and cried. Oh, the woman she is today. Wow. I am so proud of her, and we're so very close.

My journey had me standing in lines at county jails more often than I can count, to visit my own children. I never felt scared or uncomfortable, in fact, I felt like I belonged there. I was always having conversations with other parents, and God was always speaking to them through the study He'd given me earlier in the day, and often in ways I still can't explain. He speaks through me, I don't have those words. One day our church announced that we were starting a prison ministry, and I knew that's what I was supposed to do.

I've been working with inmates in county and state jails and prisons for several years now. I share my stories with women who behaved like I did, only they got caught. I realize what a blessing it was to learn my lessons out here, to be able to pray from the outside of those walls. These incredible women feel so lost and saddened, and I know what if feels like to believe you've failed your children, failed your God. I can experience not only sympathy, but empathy for them. I can love them like I love myself.

Our God is about reconciliation. Our Jesus is about healing. The Holy Spirit indeed leads us into ALL truth, and without the Godhead active in our lives, the pain we experience is just Satan-fodder, and it's crippling. I now understand that I was made for this specific moment in time, not to fail, but to rise. The willing and obedient eat the fat of the land. I am both. That's the I AM in me.

No good soldier lives a soft life. I've been taught to fight. My sword is the Word of God.

He loved me when I was yet in my sin, and the offspring of the Righteous are blessed. I'm the Righteousness of God in Christ by faith, so my children are blessed. I don't speak my circumstance anymore, I speak only TRUTH, found in the Word of God. The Truth is, He's not done with my kids and He's NEVER left me or forsaken me or left me an orphan. The Truth is, this is the generation we were warned about (2 Timothy) and their kids will have even more to contend with. Do we watch in horror? Or do we take a soldier's stance and pray vigilantly?

I say a weapon in one hand and a tool in the other, side by side as we rebuild our Jerusalems. (Neh 4)

Because God does hear our prayers, and He **is** mighty to save, and He **is** on my side. His desire is FOR us, and His will is that none would be lost, *including my kids*. We don't have time to ignore the very real call on our lives.

Jesus saw throngs of people—think rock concerts or gangs—and said the harvest was plentiful but the laborers were few. Pray to the God of the harvest to thrust laborers forth. That's you, that's me, and since God **always** causes us to triumph, it's time to get moving.

What is He calling you to do? Don't ignore it for a second. My life with Him has made all the difference in the way I get to experience life, and I love sharing it every chance I get. This is an adventure, a thrill ride, and if we determine to prepare ourselves, this is a life worth giving.

Dangerous Times and Oblivious Parenting

Susan Hamilton

Faith from My Own Perspective

Sue Batton Leonard

Isn't it interesting how we all come to our faith (or not) and our understanding of a higher being differently? I find that compelling. When I look back at my life, I suppose I am a slow learner because I didn't understand faith's power and presence until I sat down to write my award-winning memoir *Gift of a Lifetime: Finding Fulfilling Things in the Unexpected*.

With each chapter I wrote, I came to a deeper understanding of how God has been with me all the time, and I never fully recognized it. Perhaps I was too busy living life, and had never reflected upon His impact.

Now I see my journey with God began from my inception and even more apparently from the moment of my birth. As a pioneering heart patient, I was never expected to live, however, I did. Somehow just the right people I needed in my life for survival were there for me and had an unwillingness to give up. Medical researchers and doctors with bright ideas, surgeons with skilled hands, parents full of faith, hope and positive attitudes. Siblings and grandparents who helped me along the journey to a healthy recovery.

Another very special person's path crossed with mine. She turned my frowns into laughter and has continued to inspire me even today, although she is gone to be with her Creator. She taught me vital life lessons I ordinarily would not have listened to as a child if they had come from my parents. Setting an inspirational example, she shared her perspective which opened my eyes to unique ways of thinking about faith and myself. Her gospel truth from an African American perspective lead me to accept and understand we are all God's people with unique talents and gifts even though we may practice different denominations of Christianity.

Through my writing I have had an epiphany of large proportions. I have discovered I have been given the greatest gift of all—life and my own creativity, which I had never explored before. I look at life very differently now than I used to. Without having written a memoir and my newest publication, *Sew the Heart*, I don't know when I would have come to understand the present. Perhaps in the next huge challenge that life holds for me? Or maybe through my next walk in nature?

I've always known I was blessed having lived through my early years but now I understand the magnification of what I have been given more fully. With each chapter I wrote in my anthology of stories there were lessons for me from God. In fact, even though my early years have long passed, I now realize every difficult time then and from here on out will have something valuable in it for me. In seeking the lessons I will find more truths about faith. I've come to understand that's how life is designed. In retrospect I see faith has played an important role in both difficult and joyful times in my life. I can recite few Bible passages and I certainly don't have great familiarity with the stories in the big tome that contains the word of God and the prophets. But I have real experiences whereby I have very deeply felt God's presence now that I have reflected on it through my writing.

The reality is so few people who say they are going to write a book finish them and get them published. It is not an easy task, whether you have an agent and a contract with a publishing company or decide to go the independent route. But, I felt confident if I didn't lose sight of my new found faith, I'd get through the publishing process. Again, just the right people were there for me when I needed them. And there was a bonus along my creative route towards self-discovery! I learned I love to write and share my knowledge about the industry of independent publishing.

And you know what? An author's work isn't unique because as human beings we all have career choices which come with emotions, feelings, joy, strife and struggle. In order to succeed at anything we must help ourselves and do the necessary "inner" work.

Let's be clear. Having faith does not get anyone off the hook from doing the requisite work of self-improvement and reflection. The hard work must come from within us. Only we can create the kind of life we want for ourselves.

Life presents itself differently to each one of us it, we can all be sure of that. For some the road is rockier than others with more stones to trip on along the way. Some of us have to pick ourselves up from the depths of despair many more times than others. What's important is that we look for the gifts, the treasure, in every situation.

I've come to recognize struggle is part of all our life stories and have come to an understanding within myself. Living with faith has made a difference in my life. I am grateful to have awareness so I will remember to keep faith front and center.

The good news is, with every challenge from here on, I'll come out the other side a stronger person and gain life skills I didn't previously have. Various career paths, relationships with people, times of fulfillment and loss, and other bumps and bruises along the road of life make us better people. With faith, surviving and thriving comes much more easily and it comforts us.

Consider it pure joy, my brothers and sisters, whenever you face trials of many kinds, because you know that the testing of your faith produces perseverance. Let perseverance finish its work so that you may be mature and complete, not lacking anything. ~ James 1:2-4

Life is a work in progress and so is writing. I am so very grateful for them both.

Gift of a Lifetime: Finding Fulfilling Things in the Unexpected and *Sew the Heart* are available through online bookstores.

Sue Batton Leonard

Too Many Mistakes

Therese Shelesky

The stall in the women's restroom at my place of employment was a place of letting go, a place of comfort where I could release my tears and my bundled up anxiety, a place of seclusion for peace and rest. I didn't hate my job or anyone at the workplace. My tears and anxiety had to do with my dreadful personal life. Like in the past, I wanted to run, hide, and escape the painful agony of feeling hurt and defeated. I couldn't believe these feelings persisted. I thought things would be different this time; I was older, a little wiser and yet nothing was different. The baggage of my distant past, as well as the more recent past, was influencing my life in the present.

The distant past included a dysfunctional childhood. It consisted of arguing parents trying to do life together and make a way for their children. It was about being placed in nursery school or with babysitters while parents worked or were in need of breathing space. It included memories of a neighbor, who was an occasional caretaker and an abusive woman. Even today, I find myself in a state of anger or panic when grabbed, restrained or challenged by a similar female personality. Like most of us, several early childhood memories are filed away in my memory bank and are hard to forget. Although there were good times in my childhood as well, those times tend to get clouded by the difficult times and cause issues for my mind.

The recent past includes marriages, divorces, abandonment of my child due to a controlling ex-husband, a couple of unplanned and terminated pregnancies, many jobs in many states, an estranged daughter, and different residences. Introspectively, it was looking for love in all the wrong places: marriages, adultery, work, and acquiring numerous pets. It included the use of alcohol, frequenting nightclubs and many purchases to help get through each week. It also included a third and final marriage that created a blended family, more extended family, along with the continuation and additional domestic court hearings as well as more stress and health issues.

Today I am a woman in transformation. Not a perfect woman, but a woman who slowly accepts the past. A woman who is trying to live in the present irrespective of its challenges, who knows there is always the unforeseen, yet has hope for the future. I can now accept the ongoing transformation of my mind, the continuous healing of my heart and my body's health issues. Before I share why today is new, who is behind the transformation, my hope and redefining my life, let me take you back to where it all began…back to the stall in the women's restroom at my former place of employment.

In the third year of my third marriage I hit a wall and began a downward spiral emotionally and physically. I was very familiar with this spiral. I had experienced it many times before due to poor choices, my mistakes, and the decisions, words and actions of others. I was striving, but not thriving. I was striving to be a good wife, knowing that I had failed twice before. I was striving to be a better Mom, because I had abandoned my daughter for nine months. I was striving to be a good step-parent with two new little ones in my life. I was striving to be a good daughter, trying to make up for my many past failures, as well as a better daughter-in-law, since I had failed twice before and was having a difficult start the third time around. I was striving to be a better sister, sister-in-law, and aunt, because logistically there were many miles between us. I was striving to stay healthy, understanding the toll that stress had taken on me emotionally and physically. The goal? To be better than what I was in the past. Striving for this goal was important to me. Trying to live and be better than my past on my own strength, or what was left of it, was challenging. The mistakes, poor choices and consequences along with internal guilt and shame were too much for me. My past could not be erased. It was what it was, and there was no rewind or reset button to press.

Divorce and remarriage have consequences with a broad impact. My husband and I were instant parents of an instant blended family. The blended family came with an existing blended mess. That blended mess impacted our marriage, our kids from our former marriages, and every extended family member involved. Life was exhausting, painful and full of hurt that led to anger, followed by bitterness.

In January of 2003, we were in the midst of two domestic court cases. Mine, with my daughter's father, and my husband with his children's mother. The outcome of my case was devastating. My daughter chose not to continue visits and desired that the relationship be severed, which included my parents and immediate family. The pain was deep. I failed as a parent and was rejected by my one and only child. The outcome was so devastating that I could no longer do life as I used to. The stall in the women's restroom at my place of employment was no longer enough for me to keep it together. I gave my two-week notice.

The outcome of my husband's case led to several years filled with court hearings, a number of attorneys, several therapists and a custody evaluation that brought my past to the forefront. The custody evaluation results not only revealed the cause of my daughter estranging herself from me, but also exposed the fact that others had interfered with the relationship between my daughter and me. The domestic battle between my husband and his ex-wife escalated an extended family conflict that was too difficult to manage. The family division was always high and excruciatingly painful. A few weeks after each of our hearings, my cat of fifteen years died. January of 2003 was neither a good month nor a good start for a new year.

The months that followed were about getting it together. I was trying to live on my own strength, but still not succeeding. I filled my days with volunteering my time for good causes like CASA (Court Appointed Special Advocate for Children's domestic cases) and CAFB (Capital Area Food Bank). In spite of my efforts to be a better person and serve good causes, the past and its failures brought guilt and shame. I could not reach my expectations, or the expectations of others, as a wife, step-parent or family member. Oppressed by those who believed I deliberately used and hurt them, I suffered from the unintended consequences. Life was about living on eggshells, second-guessing myself, feeling unworthy and living in defeat. No matter how I tried to right the wrongs in my life, I couldn't change anything. My efforts were not making anything better and, in some cases, it made things worse. I was tired, unhealthy, depressed, and overwhelmed. Anxiety, fear, rejection and loss created anger that lived under my skin and pierced my heart with bitterness. Like many times before, I found myself backed up against a wall and trapped. Unable to make change, I eventually hit default mode: pretend I'm okay, run from what hurts, and emotionally hide.

The problem? This time around there was no way to pretend. I was not fine. There was no place to run unless I chose to get another divorce and leave the husband I loved. My life was fully exposed and I could no longer start over and make everything disappear. Painful things that were buried had been dredged up and were alive again. I was who I was, and it was what it was. All I could do was emotionally hide in my bedroom behind a closed door.

Regardless of the occasional fun times, existing in the midst of it all like an elephant in the room, were lost relationships, family division, and profound unhappiness. Everything wore me thin. I was unfulfilled without a job, even with the volunteer work. I wasn't well enough to work and felt discontent regardless of material possessions. I was moody, short tempered, and controlling in my ways. I couldn't control my life circumstances. I was a bird in a Plexiglas birdcage, trapped, low on oxygen, and suffering as I needed to breath, and I desired freedom. I wanted everything to go away!

My birthday arrived, meaning another year had passed. Each month that passed thereafter was filled with sad situations. I lived without purpose. I fought depression. I looked at my life and would drift into dark places. A feeling of being worthless, feeling useless and being hopeless filled my mind. I remember looking up into the sky and saying, "If there is a God up there, you need to show me that you exist. I can't live like this anymore!"

Therese Shelesky

While on the phone catching up with my dad, he mentioned that he read a book called *The Purpose Driven Life*, written by Rick Warren. My father suggested that I read the book. I bought the book and read the first sentence after the table of contents. *"This is more than a book; it is a guide to a forty-day spiritual journey that will enable you to discover the answer to life's most important question: 'What on earth am I here for?' By the end of this journey you will know God's purpose for your life and will understand the big picture—how all the pieces of your life fit together."* Page after page, I became filled with knowledge and truth of who God is, the meaning of His Word (the Bible), who His Son Jesus is and the purpose of His birth, death and resurrection. After I completed the book I found a new understanding on life. All of the conventional measures that were previously important, such as happiness, family, career and ambitions, were not life's purpose. I was born by and for God's purpose!

Although there were negative events taking place in my life, I realized that I was born by God for His purpose. Everything in my life, mistakes and all, had purpose. My whole life was, is and will always be, used for good by God. That is not the message of the world we live in. The world teaches us that everything is about us. After I found this new understanding on life, I found a new mindset along with the beginning of a transformation for my mind and heart.

I studied the Bible and soaked up Christian resources and speakers who followed Jesus. I learned that Jesus was my redeemer, who took all my mistakes to the cross and disposed of them forever! I learned that I was reconciled to God in a relationship. It was hard to comprehend at the time for I had thought that a relationship with God was for priests, pastors and reverends. I also learned that Jesus, through God's Word and through my life journey, would teach me what "relationship" was with Him, God the Father and all who surrounded me here on earth. I found out that I had a real life mission and that it was a continuation of Jesus' mission on earth. The new information held freedom, purpose, fulfillment and a brighter future. The information was good news wrapped with love into one gift. The gift of Jesus Christ! The truth and simplicity of this gift of love is God's grace as referred to in John 3:16,

For God so loved the world, that He gave His only Son, that whoever believes in him should not perish but have eternal life. And John 15:12-13, *My command is this: Love each other as I have loved you. Greater love has no one than this: to lay down one's life for one's friend."*

Looking back at my life, I realized that it had been consumed by all my mistakes and poor choices, and also the continuous effort to strive in my own strength. My failures and fears had me focused on pretending, running and hiding. This led to fear and anxiety. Underneath it all was guilt and shame. I was caught up in hurt, pain and loss. I thought I was protecting myself, and at times those I loved, but I was actually in the way of my life and the ones I loved.

Once I got out of the way and allowed God to lead me, I found myself starting down a path of healing, forgiving both myself and others. I was learning how to do life from God's perspective, Jesus focused, and with love and grace. I attended church and desired ministry. Soon I became a small group leader for women with broken hearts and in broken relationships. From there I was asked to lead a prayer ministry. Four years later the Lord moved me to another church where I mentored young women, served as a small group coach and participated in church community groups. My life story was being used for good, for building God's Kingdom and for encouragement and healing others who were hurt and in pain. My faith, belief and trust in a holy, just, good, loving, forgiving and faithful God was growing in leaps and bounds. Though life was chaotic on the home front, Jesus led the way and I followed Him to the best of my ability. What I didn't know at the time was that the past would resurface and bring an important message with it.

In 2012 my husband and I moved to Steamboat Springs, Colorado. We were empty nesters with hopes to get a fresh, new start. It was scary and exciting all at the same time. Steamboat Springs had always been a fun place that my husband and I enjoyed. It was a place we loved, a place for vacationing, fond memories, and a place of retreat. It was a location where my quiet times with God were deep, full of teachings, enlightening and amazing. However, visiting and vacationing somewhere proved to be different from day to day living.

My personal expectations at that time were that our radical move to Colorado would be new, life changing, and exciting. My hopes were that it would be a chance to make a difference in lives, to grow in my marriage, to get healthy and in shape, and to grow even closer to God. Overall, I thought it would be a chance to grow personally, physically, spiritually, and emotionally. God had a plan. Steamboat Springs, Colorado, would be the place where I would be challenged spiritually and experience a deeper healing from my past. Relationships that included hurt, pain, loss, and rejection were going to play a significant role.

After living in Steamboat Springs for over a year, I found myself spiritually evaporated. I longed for my old church, my old strong Jesus believing friends and my old spiritual support system. I longed for the old, accepting, non-judgmental relationships and participating in the old ministries at my former church. Ironically, everything I longed for from a spiritual perspective was on the East coast as well as what I escaped from, the pain of extended family conflict. I could not believe that with all God's creation and an abundance of churches around me I found myself in the wilderness and spiritually dry. In spite of the many amazing outdoor activities available and the various new friendships that I made, I was unfulfilled, discontent and felt alone. I was in God's Word, attending a local church and trying my best to serve in ministry.

I found myself in the striving position again. How did this happen? Why was this happening? What happened to my freedom in Christ? Was this a testing of my faith? Was this a form of spiritual warfare? Was I truly transformed in Christ? Was I too distracted by my environment? Did I lack focus on Jesus? Was I relying on people instead of trusting God? Was it all of the above? I was baffled. After much prayer, times of waiting on God, and an accumulation of spiritual notes and Bible verses placed in a manila folder, God spoke. Create a women's ministry and name it "Women of The Way Ministries." I slowly learned that God wanted me to *let go of the old and focus on the new* (Isaiah 4:19).

In a seven-month period the Lord brought writers and volunteers, not only from Steamboat Springs but also throughout the country, and from within my family and extended family. The ministry was up and running by November of 2013. It was a testimony of God's guidance, provision and faithfulness. It was amazing! However, something was still off within me and the three years to come would explain why. My past would raise its ugly head once again and this time I found myself in a new stall to release my tears, my horse's barn stall.

As family relationships challenged me in the past, the relationships that surrounded me in Steamboat Springs did the same. Whether it was a neighbor, church folks, friends I enjoyed interests with, or friends of ministry, the relationships started out great, but then brought confusion, eventually hurt and sometimes loss. I found myself desiring to overcompensate or give generously in order to be accepted or simply keep the peace. No matter how hard I tried to make changes, whether personal or circumstantial, each situation brought challenges that were followed by some type of pain. I prayed over each situation, each relationship, each change, and each challenge. I asked God to show me what I could do differently. I received no answers. Then the ultimate relationship challenge came, a family member would come to live in our home, and I was the last to know.

They call it PTSD, Post-Traumatic Stress Disorder. I believed that this could only happen to those who experienced extreme things like war, death, rape, severe illness, or sudden loss of a loved one through death. What I learned is that any type of traumatic experience or loss can cause some type of post-traumatic stress. One might not have the full-blown disorder but may be similarly affected because of an inability to face something again that they had faced in the past. Fear, feeling unprotected, rejection, loss or failure, had been and remain, trauma buttons for my life. For me, family and extended family can press those trauma buttons, and trigger memories of experiences that I don't want to face again. Overall, personal relationships make me vulnerable to a path of hurt, loss and failure.

The temporary living situation brought with it flashbacks of the past. I felt hurt, unprotected, rejected and alone. I was angry. I couldn't do it, I didn't want to do it and I was in fight or flight mode. A state of panic came over me and I couldn't sleep at night. I had full blown anxiety. That old feeling of hopelessness had crept in. The revelation? There was a need for more healing. There was an objective to obtain, to release everything and experience FULL freedom. I was still reacting and not acting in the freedom of Christ. I was not at peace. I did not have rest, and I was not experiencing joy. The past, from the age of four to the present was brought to the forefront. I was stuck. I could not move forward alone and needed to reach out to a Christian counselor. Through an Integrated Life program, the counselor and I walked through the past. We attacked many of the skeletons and demons that were in my closet. Through that process, some were conquered and some were not. In the midst of the counseling, the challenges of painful relationships continued. Whether it was marriage, family or friends, I was hurting again. I cried out to God and remembered saying, "I know you exist. I have experienced your power. I have experienced answers to many prayers. I know I am trying to do your will and live life according to your way and through your Son. But, for the life of me, I don't understand what you are trying to teach me through all of these hurtful, painful relationships." God spoke through His Word and devotional resources. The message was clear, I needed to listen and the Holy Spirit reminded me that some conquering is meant to walk through with a counselor and others are to walk directly with the Mighty Counselor and Prince of Peace, JESUS.

"<u>I AM</u> the most important relationship. <u>Through Me</u> all things will be worked for the good. <u>Focus on Me</u> and <u>bring Me</u> your fears, your anxieties, your complaint, your upset, your pain, and your broken relationships. Pray and <u>release them to Me</u> and I will give you rest. You will have peace. You will <u>move forward in Me</u>. And, above all be <u>obedient to My Word</u> and whatever I request of you. <u>In Me</u> you will heal, you will move forward, and you will <u>find Me</u> in all circumstances. <u>Focus on Me</u> and you will not be weary and react. <u>Focus on Me</u> for you will find rest and <u>act in the freedom of My Son, JESUS</u>. Be aware when <u>My Spirit is speaking to you</u>, when to talk or act and when to be silent and be still. Be alert, for the enemy will continue to try to divide you from <u>Me</u> and from others and will try to tempt you to sin. Have grace for all as I have grace for you. Forgive all as I have forgiven you. Everything happens according to <u>My will</u>. You will fail at times, but you will also grow as you <u>abide in My Son</u> and I in <u>Him</u>. Find joy in <u>My Son, My Word</u> and <u>in My Salvation</u>. Do not allow the things of this world to distract you from <u>Me</u>. Remember to rejoice in each day <u>regardless of what it holds for you. I am with you always</u>."

By the power of the Holy Spirit, the verses below were brought to my attention while trudging through my challenging relationships and circumstances. The Lord brought the FULL message together as I trudged through the challenge of writing this chapter.

<u>Matthew 22:37-49</u>, Jesus replied, "Love the Lord your God with all your heart and with all your soul and with all your mind. This is the first and greatest commandment. And the second is like it: Love your neighbor as yourself."

<u>Psalm 46:10</u>, Be still and know that I am God; I will be exalted among the nations, I will be exalted in the earth.

<u>Matthew 11:28</u>, Come to Me, all who are weary and burdened, and I will give you rest.

<u>John 15:4-5</u>, Abide in Me, and I in you. As the branch cannot bear fruit of itself unless it abides in the vine, so neither can you unless you abide in Me. I am the vine; you are the branches. Whoever abides in me and I in him, he it is that bears much fruit, for apart from me you can do nothing.

<u>2 Corinthians 12:9a</u>, But He said to me, "My grace is sufficient for you, for my power is made perfect in weakness."

<u>Proverbs 18:21</u>, The tongue can bring death or life; those who love to talk will reap consequences.

<u>Romans 8:28</u>, And we know that in all things God works for the good of those who love Him, who have been called according to His purpose.

<u>Jeremiah 7:23</u>, But this is what I commanded them saying, 'Obey My voice and I will be your God and you will be My people and you will walk in all the way which I command you that it may be well with you.

<u>Psalm 34:4-5</u>, I sought the Lord, and He answered me; He delivered me from all my fears. Those who look to Him are radiant; their faces are never covered with shame.

<u>1 Thessalonians 5:18</u>, Give thanks in every circumstance, for this is God's will for you in Christ Jesus.

Psalm 119:143, *Trouble and distress have come upon me, but your commands give me delight.*

James 4:7-8, *Submit yourselves therefore to God. Resist the devil and he will flee from you. Draw near to God and He will draw near to you. Cleanse your hands you sinners and purify your hearts you double-minded.*

Isaiah 41:10, *So do not fear for I am with you; do not be dismayed for I am your God. I will strengthen you and help you; I will uphold you with my righteous right hand.*

Needless to say, having that family member temporarily live with my husband and me was a Godsend. It was good and necessary for my healing and growth, as well as the healing and growth of the relationship with that family member. The temporary living situation turned out better than I had expected and I'm thankful to God for the experience.

God is loving, good, trustworthy, and faithful! He will transform, test and restore us a little at a time. He knows how much we can bear and gives us strength to endure. His Word confirms this in Philippians 4:13, 1 Peter 5:10, James 1:2-4, 2 Corinthians 4:8-9 and 1 Corinthians 10:13. God will use challenging relationships and circumstances not only for our good, growth and healing, but also for the good, growth and healing of others, as referred to in 2 Corinthians 1:4 in the Bible. This is the mission and message of this book. Each writer has been wounded, is healing and desires to share their story so that others can have hope, be encouraged and find healing through Christ.

Irrespective of the amount of time I spend in God's Word and in prayer, I am human and need to be reminded that I am no different to those whose life stories are found in God's Word. These lives rose, fell, and rose again according to God's will and purpose. I will have good and bad days. I will get hurt, need to forgive, hurt others, and need to ask for their forgiveness. Life, even at this very moment is difficult and it isn't easy to accept the curve balls that come at any given time. However, through prayer, guidance from God's Word, and knowing that Jesus is always with me, I will endure, my faith will grow, and God's grace will be sufficient to get me through.

My joy? God showed me His love and protection through the gift of His Son Jesus! God gave me grace through faith in His Son Jesus and saved me, regardless of all my mistakes. Jesus gave up His life in order to give me freedom and life! This kind of love, forgiveness, grace, mercy, and protection is breathtaking and life giving!

In the midst of life and all it throws, I shall never forget that (1) I was born by and for God's purpose, (2) Jesus died for my "Too Many Mistakes," (3) I am a daughter of the King, (4) I am never alone because Jesus is always with me, and, (5) because of **JESUS** I am redeemed, reconciled in a relationship with God and my life after this will forever be with Him in His Kingdom...*where there is no more hurt, no more pain, no more fears, no more illness or disease, no more tears, no more division, no more striving, and, most of all, <u>no more mistakes</u>!*

Therese Shelesky

The Darkest Journey: Finding God's Light After Your Child's Death

Tammy Stewart

Good people pass away; the Godly often die before their time. But no one seems to care or wonder why. No one seems to understand that God is protecting them from the evil to come. Isaiah 57:1

My darkest journey began on October 26, 2009 when my son, Ryan Stewart Allen, was unexpectedly and tragically called home to Heaven. He was born on September 18, 1993 and had just turned sixteen years old. Ryan was my light, my twin soul, a child of God with a heart for God and so many others. Full of life, laughter, young and carefree, he was best known for making people happy and laugh. There are no words to describe the love I feel for this child; it can only be understood from the heart.

Let me take you back to the beginning. Ryan was born on a beautiful fall day in Redlands, California. He joined his older sister, Shilah, who was three, and made our family perfect. He grew up to be very athletic, getting a red/black belt in Tae Kwan Do at age eleven, and excelling at snowboarding, skateboarding and skiing. He also played football from middle school through high school. He was very intelligent and was on the school honor roll consistently. His greatest quality was his love for God, his family and other people. He helped people in trouble, and always stood up for the underdog. He joined a church youth group called SK8 Church at age twelve with Shilah. They went on a mission's trip to Costa Rica with money they earned and built a skateboard park. He volunteered at World Vision to send out shoes to children in other countries. He volunteered for food drives for the poor, and was always involved in community service in our hometown, Steamboat Springs, Colorado.

About a year before his death, Ryan started getting frequent ear infections and strep throat. These were treated with antibiotics, but they were not clearing up and he missed a lot of school. The doctors decided that a tonsillectomy would clear up the constant infections and bring him back to good health. He had the tonsillectomy three days before his "death" on this earth. He had this surgery on October 23, 2009 and the day of surgery seemed to go well. I prayed with Ryan as he went into the operating room. We asked God to be with him, get him safely through the surgery, and heal him. We were so faithful and hopeful that God would use this surgery for healing. Otherwise a healthy child, he just needed to have the tonsils causing so much infection removed. God did heal Ryan, but just not in the way we had prayed for or expected. He gave Ryan the ultimate healing of going Safely Home to Jesus and his Father God with no more sickness or tears for all eternity.

There were many miracles and dreams and signs that God gave me for my comfort and His glorification over the past seven years since my son's death that are all so awesome, none of them are insignificant. The purpose of this story is to describe some of these signs and miracles.

My first miracle from God came during Ryan's two-hour surgery. I saw Jesus in the operating room. Jesus was standing to the side of Ryan and appeared to be just watching. I believed Jesus was keeping him safe, and He was, but I had no idea Jesus was also there preparing to take my little baby home with Him, soon. Things went well after his surgery, and within a day, Ryan was at home eating banana ice cream and making us all laugh with his silly jokes and love.

Two days after the surgery, there was a complication, and he was taken back to the emergency room on October 25, 2009. My second light and miracle from God came while we were in the emergency room with Ryan that last night. I was sitting at the foot of his bed as he was sleeping, and I saw Jesus watching over Ryan once again with such love. There was so much brightness in the room from Jesus. I thought once again that Jesus was there healing Ryan and watching over him. He was watching over him and healing him, but once again not in the way I had expected or prayed. Seeing Jesus was not something that had happened to me very often, before. It was truly a miracle and a comfort to me. But I believe He was there more for Ryan than for me. And of course, that is fine with this mother's heart.

We got home from the emergency room that second time at about 2:30 a.m. Ryan was in so much pain, he was screaming and crying. This was heartbreaking. Ryan was a tough little guy and very athletic. He rode his snowboard and skateboard, and rode motorcycles and played football. It took a lot for him to show tears from physical pain. I made him some soup and sat with him in his bed and watched cartoons until he got tired and could sleep. I kissed my son on the forehead, told him I loved him, and that I would check on him at least every hour. That was the last time I ever saw my son alive! What a blessing those last moments became in the future. I checked on him more than every hour and he seemed to be resting, peacefully. More medical phone calls occurred the morning of October 26, 2009 between the doctors and me, but things seemed okay at that point. It was later that afternoon that things went wrong! That became the darkest day!

I was concerned later in that morning about him not waking up, even though I was told he needed to rest. I went into his room, and my nightmare, my PTSD, my flashbacks and pain beyond comprehension began. Ryan looked like he was sleeping. He was propped up on his pillows. He had his little teddy bear in his arms. But something did not look right. I shook him and pulled the covers down and his body was slightly blue and he was non-responsive. I screamed and shook him. I was crying hysterically. There was no heartbeat, no breathing and his eyes were rolled back in his head. I could not lift him. He was six feet, one inch tall and very athletic and strong. I threw all the pillows off the bed, got him on his back, and cleared his airway. I ran to get the phone and called 911. I prayed out loud, nonstop the entire time for God to heal my son. God could heal my son and give him life. He raised Lazarus from the dead and he could save my son. I thought God would heal my son.

    I did not think he was dead. I called 911 crying and praying, but also able to act and use the life saving techniques in which I had been certified. This was only by the Grace of God. The 911 operator told me to give him two breaths. When I did, I heard gurgling in his lungs. I gave him thirty C.P.R. strokes. As I did this, fluid came out of his nose and mouth that looked like blood. I had to keep wiping our faces to do the mouth to mouth, and his body to do C.P.R. There was no breath; there was no heartbeat. HELP ME JESUS! My mouth was full of my son's bodily fluids. I know God allowed me to go through an unbearable amount of trauma, but I am also the mother who with God gave this baby his first breath, and heartbeat, and I am now the mother God allowed to experience his last breath and last heartbeat. This can be seen as a blessing and a comfort as well as a horrific event. I believe God meant it for the good of a terrible situation. I was able to hold him as he was going home to Jesus. Mother Mary was also able to hold her son as he was dead, and to have His blood on her body. God blessed me in the same way He blessed the Mother of God. Romans 8:28: *We know that in all things God works for the good of those who love Him.*

    The First Responders arrive after about twenty minutes. I am still praying out loud harder than I have ever prayed in my life and doing C.P.R. and believe God is going to save him. The alternative was too unbearable. They did everything they could to revive him, and then put him in the ambulance. I knew God was the only one who could save my baby. I felt I was all alone, but know God was with me. I made all the telephone calls to family from the ambulance. The worst was to my daughter, Shilah, who was at college eight hours away. They were so close and talked or texted every day. I didn't know how to get her here quickly or if she could survive what was about to occur.

    The hospital was a nightmare, truly. Ryan's friends, his youth group, were there crying, and screaming. Pastors were trying to comfort us but were shell shocked themselves. I was forced into a room, alone, away from everyone, and away from Ryan. I screamed and cried and prayed, and I wanted to die. I could not breathe. Where is God, I wondered? *Then Jesus wept.* John 11:35. A doctor then came into the little room on October 26, 2009 at 14:06 p.m., Shilah was on the phone. We were told Ryan was dead and they could not save him. I did not believe it. Jesus was going to save him, right? I hear screaming and see only blackness.

I was soon allowed to go see my baby boy for that last time while at the hospital. It was his body, but now just a shell. His spirit is in heaven and he is saved and has eternal life. But I see the body I have loved for sixteen years and do not want to let go. I hold him, kiss him, and cut a piece of his beautiful blonde hair. A body is better than no son at all. The assistant coroner is a kind, Godly man and lets me stay for hours before he must take him. How do you say goodbye and just walk out? Ryan has to go to Denver for an autopsy and won't be back for several days. So now not even a body for me to cling to. I refuse to say goodbye because in Christ there is no goodbye! I have never said goodbye to sweet Ryan. I go home to Ryan's room and do not leave it for any real periods of time for months. It is peaceful and I am close to my son and to Jesus there. I wait for family to arrive. My life and the life of my family will never be the same. I try to accept God's decision and turn to the Bible and unceasing prayer and tears. It is the darkest day!

The impact of losing Ryan now begins for my family and me! The next week is the nightmare of planning a funeral. Only God can get a parent through that process. I want to die, but I made a promise to Ryan at the hospital that I would live for his sister, for my mother, and for my God! Prior to Ryan going home to his Savior, he had recently attended the funeral of a friend's mother. He texted me during that funeral that he loved me so much and could never live without me. He asked me to never die before him. He prayed that I would never leave him. I let him know that I prayed God would keep me alive to love and take care of him. God did answer that prayer for Ryan and for me. God knew that Ryan could not make it if I left him first, so by the grace of God He took Ryan home first.

In the week prior to Ryan going to heaven, I had an unusual vision from Jesus. I saw Ryan, Shilah and me on a rock by the river. We were sitting on the rock and facing the water. Jesus was behind us. He had His arms stretched around all three of us and was holding us close together in His protection and love. He has never let go!

God gave me miracles and signs after Ryan went to heaven, but God was preparing me in other ways for Ryan to go home prior to taking him. On my last Mother's Day with Ryan, he made me the most beautiful piece of art to treasure forever. He saved money from his job to make and pay for it. He made a photo piece that said MOM from pictures of different churches to spell out the letters, because he knew of my love for God. He also made me a table in woodworking class to keep in our house, forever. Ryan had his sixteenth birthday on September 18, 2009, about thirty-eight days before he went home. I took a picture of Ryan at his birthday dinner, and when the picture came out, there were golden rays coming down from heaven and touching Ryan. You could not see this with the naked eye, only in the developed picture. On my last birthday with Ryan on September 30, 2009, Ryan gave me an amazing birthday, like never before. He cooked a steak dinner with mashed potatoes and a homemade German chocolate cake. He had worked to earn money and did the shopping. He bought me so many gifts. He bought me a beautiful hand carved quartz humming bird. Ryan and I used to watch humming birds together in the back yard. He wrote me a card that was pure love—so loving it was the kind of card you would keep forever. What a beautiful card and what beautiful words, that would be the last I had from him until we are reunited in heaven.

As Sk8 Church, Ryan's skateboarding youth group, helped get his memorial and celebration of life ceremony together. Tara, his youth leader, came to the house with her computer to show us pictures of Ryan for a slide show. She said Ryan had recently professed Jesus Christ, but she did not think she would be able to find that video since there were hundreds on her computer from the youth group. She turned the computer on, and the computer turned on to the very video of Ryan praising Jesus she thought she would not be able to find!

God continued to give me miracles leading up to Ryan's memorial service which would be held on Halloween. The first night he was gone, and I was sleeping in his bed, I prayed and prayed for Ryan to be at peace and with God and to be happy and safe. Ryan went to youth group and church and prayed, but I needed to know. I woke up from sleeping and I heard Ryan's voice say to me three times..." I'm okay, Mom. I love you." The next night I was praying the same prayer to God, and a loud, booming voice came into my head and said, "He is already here in heaven, Tammy. You do not need to pray about that anymore!" It surely was the voice of God. During the same week, a group of very strong prayer warrior women came to my house to pray with us. I told them about the video of Ryan professing Jesus being found. One of the women, during prayer, said in a very deep and stern voice, "Ryan took it very seriously when he accepted me as his savior and I took it very seriously when he said it, and I do not waiver. Do not ever doubt this again!" Once again, surely the voice of God!

The most powerful miracle of God came from a vision He gave me. I was having horrible flashbacks and PTSD from the day I found him and could not even close my eyes without seeing all the horror. I knew only God could heal me from this memory and decided I would count on the Lord to be my physician and healer. Jesus is the ultimate healer and no one I was seeing on earth was helping me. The powerful prayer group of women from church came over and we talked about it. We got in a circle and held hands and prayed. They had me go back in my mind to Ryan's room at that terrible time and talk about what I saw and felt. I did and it was so painful. They told me then to see what Jesus saw in that room. I immediately saw a vision. I saw Ryan sitting up in his bed. His face was so light and bright and happy and full of expectation. It was not like any look I have ever seen on his face or on this earth. He had brightness and light all around him. He was smiling. He had his arms stretched out towards the end of the bed, straight out in front of him. He and his bed were clean and bright with no body fluids or sickness around him. He was holding his arms out for his Jesus who had come to get him. Jesus was there to take Ryan home! Jesus let me see this miracle to comfort this mother's heart. John 14:3 states *When everything is ready I will come and get you so you will always be with me where I am going.*

The day before the memorial service, it seemed impossible that I would be able to survive. Praise God I had my family around me, friend's around me, and a very supportive and loving city of Steamboat Springs, Colorado. Most of all, I had Jesus carrying me through it all. We had a viewing the night before the memorial service, and I spent hours holding and hugging the body of Ryan for the last time I would ever see it on this earth. I wanted to keep that body with me forever just to hold on to. He looked so beautiful to me, and was still my little Ryan. So many friends and family came to see him one last time on this earth and hold and love him.

During Ryan's memorial service at the church, which was completely packed because he was so loved by this community, and so beautiful and precious and so full of love, I literally thought I would just die. How can a mother survive all this pain and the pain of Shilah and the family? I was crying and barely breathing. Then God spoke to me and told me I needed to get up and speak to the people there. I was shocked and ignored it for a while, but God was going to have me speak. I told the pastor, who was in shock as well by my request to talk, but he let me get up with Ryan's teddy bear, Mr. Bear, to speak. God used me to talk about his love, and comfort and eternity and eternal life. I have no idea what I said, but people cried and said it was an amazing speech of God's eternal love and salvation! Another miracle from a God full of love and miracles! God's grace and mercy somehow got me through the "death," the service preparation, the viewing, and actual memorial service. The darkest journey continues with God's light and grace and comfort slipping through.

The "death" and memorial service described are blunt and hard to read. I held back on some of the more graphic and painful events, but this was the reality. It shows even more clearly how bright God's love and light can shine in such an unimaginable, unbearable and painful loss.

The weeks after the memorial service were bleak and dark and horrible to remember or to describe. It affected me, my entire family, and especially my little Shilah, and my mother. Survival for us was not guaranteed. All we could do was pray and rely on our Savior. We could read the Bible. When the words would not come, our tears spoke volumes. When you cannot even open the Bible, you can lay it on your heart, and God understands! God has never turned His back and had always been right there!

My testimony and reason for being on this earth, is to witness and testify about all the miracles, signs, dreams, visions, and the supernatural light that God has sent me since that darkest day on October 26, 2009. He has spoken to me and told me that my purpose is to glorify Him and comfort others in the same way He has comforted me in an otherwise un-survivable darkness.

God spoke to me on February 3, 2010 to testify and give comfort to others as he had comforted me. I was driving home from a long journey from my daughter's home. For months, God had been showing me a verse over and over in Bible study classes, and in church sermons and basically banging me over the head with this verse until I understood His wishes! On February 3, 2011, I finally understood. The verse was 2 Corinthians 1:3-4, *All praise to God the Father of our Lord Jesus Christ. God is our merciful Father and the source of all comfort. He comforts us in all our troubles so that we can comfort others. When they are troubled, we will be able to give them the same comfort God has given us."*

God told me to write a book about miracles, signs, dreams and visions He has given me since my Ryan was called home. Without God's love, comfort and miracles, I would not have survived my darkest journey. I obeyed God and I wrote a book published in 2013 called *The Darkest Journey, Finding God's Light During The First Year of Your Child's Death*. Without God's guidance, I did not have the ability to write the book; I was so overwrought emotionally.

God also told me to start a parent support group called "Children of God" and help people through my law practice who needed help and had no voice or financial resources to participate in the legal system. Since that day, I have had a Christian law office dedicated to Poverty Law. I did not ignore God when He asked me to do something for His glory, and He provided me with the means to do it. My life continues to follow the directions God gave me on that cold February day nearly six years ago, and I do not expect that to change.

The miracles, dreams, signs and visions God has given to me for my comfort and for His glorification over the past six years are more numerous than will fit in a book chapter. It took a complete book to record the first year of Miracles in my/God's book. I have journaled most of my adult life, and all the miracles were written at or near the time they happened. The miracles in this chapter will be highlights of the most awesome miracles, but all the miracles were awesome and such a comfort for this mother's heart that none were insignificant.

Just a month after Ryan's call home, we ate dinner at a friend's house. It was at the home of one of the powerful prayer women that had helped me so greatly in the past. We prayed and she told me that Ryan now knows Moses and Jesus and Matthew and all the saints and disciples. She prayed that God would let me see Ryan. I then saw a vision of Jesus standing on a rock in the river next to me. Little Ryan was on the next rock. He was about eight years old. He was playing and happy. I then saw Ryan on the same rock and now he was sixteen. He had his Rockies baseball hat on sideways, and a long grey tall t-shirt, and his slouchy jeans; his iPod was in his ears. He looked so happy and peaceful.

A month later, I was cleaning and just gave up and laid down on the floor and cried and stared at the ceiling. I felt Ryan close to me in my heart. He was talking to me in his own voice and words in my thoughts. He said, "Mom, it is beautiful up here." He told me Jesus came and got him. He thanked me for trying to save his life and never giving up on him in his entire life, even to the death. He told me he had seen Jesus and how he now had a Father in heaven that loves him. He told me I was right about God and heaven. He told me he loves me and he isn't that far away from me. He also said he would see me again. He told me not to feel sad about finding him in his bed because it was his favorite place. He said when I came in and found him he was already with Jesus and he was okay. He told me I was still his mom, and he was always my little boy. He told me he didn't want to die, but he was happy and he was in paradise. Job 14:5 *You have decided the length of our lives. You know how many months we will live and we are not given a minute longer.*

The day that Ryan was called home, my mother's neighbor, also a strong prayer warrior, heard from God. God told her to make a specific item for me, and wait until the right time to give it to me. She made a bracelet. Ryan's birthstone is a sapphire. The bracelet had sixteen blue sapphire beads to represent the sixteen years of Ryan's life. In the middle of the bracelet was an Opal to represent October, the month Ryan went home to God. On each side of the Opal was a bright white bead to represent the Holy Spirit that surrounded Ryan when he died. On each end of the bracelet was a bigger sapphire bead (also my birthstone) with a clear bead next to them. It represented me and the Holy Spirit that was with me when Ryan went to heaven, and the Holy Spirit that was with me when Ryan was born. There was a cross charm on it for my heart for Christ, and a heart charm on it for my love and heart for Ryan. She gave it to me for Christmas, 2009.

On New Year's Day of 2010, I woke up and was grieving and tearful and could not imagine a year that did not have Ryan in it. I prayed for comfort and peace. I know God catches every tear I cry. He feels my pain and weeps with me. I prayed and prayed for peace and to know Ryan's peace. A voice inside me (the Holy Spirit?) told me again that Ryan was with God and that he was happy and at peace. I also heard a voice inside me tell me, "I love you, mom. I am good. I am happy." Psalms 5:6-8 *You keep track of all my sorrows. You have collected all my tears in your bottle. You have recorded each one in your book.*

More miracles arrived! Precious God keeps them coming to comfort my heart and somehow keep me and Shilah and my mama going in this dark world without Ryan. It was February, 2010. I prayed for God to give me signs and dreams and visions of Jesus, heaven, and my Ryan, or whatever He needed to give me. I rarely dream of Ryan although I pray to every night. That night I had a beautiful dream of Ryan. Shilah and I were on a shore of a river, and we saw Ryan laughing and playing and jumping over the water and in the water and doing flips in the air. He went through the wall of a ship. He tells us he loves us and laughs about how great his new body is. He tells us he cannot stay long and has to go. That same day I am looking through Ryan's closet. I have left his room the same to this day. It is my prayer room and a peaceful refuge. I looked behind his snowboard and I found a small copy of his Sk8 Church Bible. It has several versed highlighted in yellow and I can read the verses Ryan loved and highlighted! One verse he had highlighted was the very reason for my writing my book. 2Corinthians 1:3-4, *we must comfort others because God has first comforted us!*

Later in February, 2010, I woke up and my hand was over the edge of the bed. I felt fingers intertwined with mine! It lasted a full five minutes, and that hand never let go. I was wide awake and not dreaming. No one else was in the room with me. It was either God or Ryan and was so comforting.

Also in February, 2010, God gave me a financial blessing and miracle that is without measure. I needed to stay in this house. I raised my children here, and there are so many beautiful memories, and their laughter echoes off the walls. I needed Ryan's room for comfort and refuge and peace. I needed to be in the last place he ever took an earthly breath. My mortgage had doubled and there was no way I could pay it. I could not get the mortgage refinanced as it was upside down. I prayed and prayed and prayed. I wrote letters to the mortgage company and talked to them and begged them to please modify my loan so I could stay in this home. It was beyond all the odds that this would happen. Banks just were not offering that option anymore. But the God in me is stronger than he in the world and the bank, due to God's intercession and miracle, modified my loan so I could manage to keep living in our family home! And I am still here, praise God!

That same summer, I noticed something odd with one of Ryan's pictures. It was one of my favorite pictures and sits on my desk where I look at it every day. He is in Costa Rica on a mission's trip with Sk8 Church. He is leaning sideways with his head on his hand, a skateboard cap on, and the most peaceful and loving expression on his face. His green eyes sparkle with love straight from his soul. I dust this picture, often. There is glass in the frame in front of the picture, as usual. I have cleaned that glass with glass cleaner. I happened to glance over at the picture. And noticed the glass was missing from the frame. The picture was still there. I asked Shilah if she accidently broke the glass, and she had no idea what I was talking about even after showing it to her. I thought maybe the cats had knocked it out somehow, but could not find any broken glass anywhere or the pane of glass either. I finally went and bought a new frame. As I was taking the picture out of the frame with no glass, there was the pane of glass behind the picture! It was not in front of the picture where it had always been, but behind the picture. There is no way that could happen without divine intervention. It was impossible. I believe it was God and Ryan showing me their continued presence, and definitely Ryan's sense of humor. Ryan loved to play silly jokes on his mom.

In July, 2010, God has given me another beautiful miracle. I receive a humming bird messenger from God! God knows the importance of humming birds to Ryan and me. We loved them together, fed them and shared watching them. It was the last birthday present he ever gave me; a hand carved quartz humming bird. Ryan knew how much I loved humming birds. That summer the humming birds were gone. Ryan was gone. I didn't know why the birds did not come anymore. One morning I was praying at Ryan's grave. I was on my knees with my hands on top of the headstone and my head bowed. I was crying and telling Ryan how much I loved and missed him. Suddenly I heard a humming bird! I opened my eyes and right in front of me, right on the top of Ryan's headstone, was a beautiful red Humming Bird. It flew there in one spot for a bit and then zipped off. It was such a sign of love and hope from God and Ryan. Thank you, dear Lord, for the miracle and that sign. I got a red humming bird tattooed on the outside of my right wrist in honor of that miracle. Ryan's name is on the top with a halo over his name.

October 26, 2010, is Ryan's first heaven birthday. The dreaded day of pain that you are not sure you can survive. But you remember that God's grace is sufficient, and His mercies are new every day, and you face it. My mom and I went to Durango to celebrate this birthday of Ryan in heaven with sweet Shilah. We bought beautiful orange and red roses, Ryan's favorite. We went to the river. Shilah told Ryan that day at the river, that the river is life and it keeps on going and moves around any obstacles. She tells him the river is peaceful just like Ryan, now. She tells Ryan he is serene, and perfect and at peace with Jesus and God in eternity. Grandma Sally tells him she loves him and misses him for his gentleness the most; and how he loved and cared so deeply for other people and animals. I told him I loved his kind heart and love for others and his beautiful loving soul. I loved how he always made me and others smile and laugh every day. I know he still does this! We told him so much more! We then threw the roses in the water one by one and said something about Ryan with each one. They gently floated downstream, out of sight, with our tears following.

After we threw the flowers and prayed and cried, a young woman drove up by the riverbank. She had one of the roses we had thrown in her hand. It floated to her downstream and she felt she needed to find where it came from and return it to somebody or back to the river. She walked toward us, and out of the blue said, "Was this for your son?" I told her yes, and she said "RYAN thinks about you all the time." She had no way of knowing it was for our son, or his name was Ryan. She was nowhere near where we were to hear, and had to drive her car all the way back until she found us. God is awesome! We thought maybe she was an angel?

These are some of the Miracles, signs, dreams and visions God blessed me with that first year with Ryan in heaven. God's mercies never end and are new every day. The rest of this chapter is the miracles and signs God continued to send me to heal, and to love and comfort me through a dark journey that will not end until I am reunited with my Ryan. But God gives sufficient grace every day and His light is brighter than any darkness. There have been many, many miracles and signs from God in the last seven years, but too many to fit in a chapter. I am highlighting some of the bigger ones. But God is still here right next to me, carrying me, and His love and miracles have never ceased and never will.

I ran a memorial ad in the local paper after Ryan's first heaven birthday. I wanted to save the photo and tribute to my computer and send it to my family. The picture the paper sent to me would not download on my computer and they could not help me. I was so upset. I tried for hours, cried, and turned the computer off and went to bed. The next morning when I woke up the computer was on, and the picture I wanted of Ryan was showing on the computer, full page, and had somehow opened in my Kodak program. Thank you, Father!

On Memorial Day of 2011, I went to Ryan's grave with flowers to spend time and pray. I had a full battery on my phone. I tried three times to take a picture of the flowers, and three times the phone went dead and the battery showed it was dead. It finally worked. I believe it was Ryan playing a silly joke on me, again. The same day, another friend went up and tried to take a picture. Her phone also turned off three times before she got a picture.

In August of 2011, Shilah called me and was upset and we prayed together. It was late at night. I was home all alone. All the lights were off upstairs. After we prayed, I went upstairs. I noticed light coming from underneath Shilah's door. I had not been in her room for weeks and the lights had not been on in her room. When I opened her door, every single light and lamp in her room was on. I believe that God and Ryan were giving us a sign that our prayers for Shilah were heard and she was being cared for.

It is the summer of 2012. Grief does not soften or heal when you lose a child. God makes it possible through His love and light to give you enough grace every day to move on and wait on the Lord. Tears still come every day, and your heart still aches with the loss. Your heart is still shattered in a million pieces, but God is the glue that holds it together, and His promises, and faithfulness and love never cease. I was feeling sad on this day in June. I was looking out to my sundeck and I noticed a beautiful golden humming bird with a bright orange neck. There are few humming birds, so I am happy to see this one. He sits on the feeder right near my screen door and does not leave the area. This humming bird stays with me for four full days and is there every time I look. It is such a sweet sign of hope from God. God also sends doves to my mom's house, but only when I visit. I love doves and they remind me of peace and God, and the Holy Spirit coming down as Jesus was baptized in the form of a dove. When I visit my mom, two doves always come and stay in a tree in her yard the whole time I am there. They coo and are just present the whole time, and anytime I look out or walk out, there they are. When I leave, she says the doves leave and do not come back again until I come back.

On Ryan's twentieth' earth birthday, we wanted to celebrate and had balloons and flowers and signs and cards and toys for his grave site. But it was raining and hailing and had been most of the day. It did not look like it was going to stop. It was important to me emotionally to put these birthday items up and celebrate him. We prayed. God answered our prayer and the sun came out and shone brightly and the rain stopped. We were able to have an hour to go to his grave and set things up and have his outside birthday party.

Cats are beautiful creatures of God, but we all know they can be a little strange at times. It was still the day of Ryan's twentieth earth birthday. We were home cooking steaks and mashed potatoes for Ryan. That is our custom on his earth and heaven birthdays because it was his favorite meal. I went by Ryan's room upstairs, and both of our cats were in his room, sitting on the floor and staring at the pictures of him on his desk. They were staring and meowing. I asked them what they were doing, and they turned and looked at me, and then stared at the pictures on the desk again and just meowed. Of course, the Kitties miss and love Ryan, too.

Living everyday with this grief is so hard, but God always knows when I need comfort from Him. I had to have some medical tests in the same hospital Ryan had previously had the same tests done in Denver. It was so emotional to go into any hospital after the way Ryan died, but to go to the same hospital for the same test was agony. I cried the whole time and am sure the doctors just thought I was crazy. I prayed for strength and comfort during a specific test that lasted about an hour, and Jesus' voice in my head told me he was with me. And then I heard Ryan tell me he would do the test for me. I told him, no, it had to be my test results, but for the next hour I had Jesus and my son with me and I had no stress at all.

In September 2014, my family and I attended a religious convention with a well-known pastor and healer. It was a three-day seminar and we were given so many signs during that time. At one time, I was praying for comfort and healing and just thinking of my beautiful Ryan. I heard a voice speak to me and say, "He is okay, he is okay. Ryan is happy. Ryan is in heaven." I do know he is in heaven and he is happy, and I am so thankful God has saved my son and he will spend eternity with Jesus and Father God in paradise. But my heart still hurts without him, and I will not be whole again until we are reunited. I am so thankful for these continued gifts from God. He heals and comforts and loves and is always present! I would not be here today without the love and comfort and healing He has given. But there will be complete healing in heaven, and until then, God sustains me with His loving signs and miracles.

September 30, 2014 is another of my favorite gifts from God. I was with Ryan's previous girlfriend and we were together on my birthday. She was moving out of state and wanted to say goodbye and see and take pictures of Ryan's room and house again before she left. We were talking about Ryan being saved and heaven, and she mentioned she had a picture Ryan made in Photoshop just weeks before he died. It was a picture of Jesus! For five years, I had no idea it existed. She brought it over to me and it was the most beautiful and amazing picture I had ever seen. It is a picture of Jesus in a white robe with a red waist and red cuffs, and red around the neck. His face shines with love. His face and hair are just like the Jesus I picture and imagine. In the picture He is walking toward us through a field of bright yellow sunflowers. His palms are facing up and out toward us. Everywhere He has walked, the sunflowers are yellow and full of color. The flowers around Him where he has not yet stepped are in black and white with no color. There is a beautiful mountain scene behind him and a beautiful sky. Jesus brings light to the world is what I think of when I see the picture. It was delivered to me five years after the best and last birthday I ever had with my Ryan. What a beautiful birthday present from God and from my son!

In November, 2014, I was dusting in Ryan's room, missing him and just loving looking at all the precious things that made his room his. I was talking to him as I dusted. Suddenly the smoke detector in his room started beeping. It beeped the entire time I was in the room. When I left the room, the beeping stopped immediately. It was my Ryan talking to me. Another time, I was in Ryan's room in the dark to pray. As I was praying I felt a light come on. I opened my eyes and his cell phone on his night stand was lighting up like it does when someone calls, and then going out. There were no calls or messages coming in, and the phone lit up and off the entire time I was in the room. It stopped when I left the room.

One day in February of 2015 was a rainy, teary day. I missed my Ryan and stopped at the cemetery to visit him. I was kneeling in the overcast, rainy sky praying. My eyes were closed. I then felt the sunshine come out and shine on my face and warm me. I could see the light behind my closed eyes and feel the warmth on my upturned face. I was so thankful for such a beautiful sign from God. I continued to pray and feel the warmth. I opened my eyes, and the sun was not out! It was cloudy and cold and rainy. God gave me the gift of the Sonshine.

It is May, 2015. This is a miracle from God for all our family. Shilah was so close to Ryan and his death nearly destroyed her. I can only say she figuratively went to hell and back in the six years since he died. His death affected her mental, emotional, and physical health. School was a struggle and it took her six years to graduate due to Ryan leaving us. It is her story to tell, but I can say God restored her and redeemed her and healed her. Nothing would make Ryan happier (or me!). Shilah, after six years of struggling with all her will and might and prayers, graduated with her Bachelor of Science degree in Environmental Biology with honors! She has done four internships in Wildlife Biology and is a beautiful daughter of God! God continues to pour His blessings down on her, and she is walking a closer walk with God.

Near the same time, I was feeling sad, and crying and praying and writing poetry. I just wanted to see and hold my Ryan. I decided to go to Facebook and see cute pictures of animals and scriptures to help me cheer up. I turned on Facebook, and the very first thing that came up was a brand-new picture I had never seen before of my Ryan. His girlfriend had posted it. It was a picture taken right before he died, and he was standing and petting her dog. He was so tall and handsome and had so much love on his face for the dog, with that sweet little smile he has. I cried from happiness. A new picture of my son I had not seen, and God's love comforting me again.

Another day in the fall of 2015, I was feeling sad and broken and needed God. I went into Ryan's room, my peaceful sanctuary. I asked God to give me peace that surpasses all understanding. I prayed deeply for this peace. And there it was. My cats were snuggled up next to me in Ryan's bed. Ryan's little Teddy Bear was in my arms, and a peace like no other came over me. It did surpass all understanding. I felt peace, and rest. There was no pain and pure love from my Savior and Ryan. I felt a small part of the love and comfort and peace that Ryan would be feeling everyday times one thousand-fold. I knew God was taking care of my mom and daughter and husband. He had me close in His arms. It was a small bit of perfect peace and what I believe is to come for eternity. It was like a dream, a vision, and an out of body experience. It was a feeling I never wanted to end.

October 31, 2015 was the sixth anniversary of Ryan's burial. I was cold and sad and broken. I gave it to God in prayer. He knows my pain. He saw His son suffer and die, and it broke God's heart as well. He whispers to me that He is with me, and He understands, and feels the pain of my heart and grief. He is a healer, and I can move on, like so many times before when God meets my pain with His love.

God is with me always, and in November 2015, I had an incredible dream like no other. I was in bed and could not sleep. I was praying to God and praising Him and asking for His peace and rest for my broken body and heart. He hears me and He answers me. I fall asleep. The peace is indescribable. I feel I am in heaven and I see Jesus who is there to meet me. His face is so beautiful and so full of love. He was all love, and all good. Ryan was there and so happy to see me. He was beautiful and bright and shining. He showed me his new body and all the cool things he could do with it like run so fast and jump in the air, and put his hand through a wall. He hugged me and told me time was different there. There was no sense of waiting for me, or of loss. He remembered me just seconds before that being with him, and some short time ago talking to me, and I was here with him, now. All my heaven relatives were there, and they loved Ryan and me so much. Ryan told me about all the exciting people he had met. He showed me around a small portion of heaven. It was perfect peace and love. He showed me a wolf lying with a lamb (he knows how much I love wolves). He showed me delicious fruit and clear, sparkling water. He held my hand and led me. Jesus was always close by. I heard beautiful singing and praises to God. I know our treasures lie in heaven and they will be more than eye has seen or ear has heard. I try to wait patiently for that day and my Lord. This was a treasure to hold on to until that day comes.

Life has been so hard for me and my mother and daughter since God took Ryan. I still cry every day. My mother cries for him and for me. My daughter continues to struggle with the pain but now has a closer walk with God and more peace that Ryan is in paradise. We celebrate his earth birthday and heaven birthday every year. We must rely on a stronger faith in God to survive, and God has given us all His grace that we need, now. God's words sustain me. *You saw me before I was born. Every day of my life was recorded in your book. Every moment was laid out before a single day had passed.* Psalms 139:16 This verse has probably sustained me more than any other verse since Ryan was called safely home. I often put Ryan's name where it says, "I." You saw Ryan before he was born. Every day of Ryan's life was recorded in your book. Every moment was laid out for Ryan before a single day had passed.

One of the highlighted verses in Ryan's Bible was James 4:7-8 *Dear brothers and sisters. Be patient as you wait for the Lord's return. Consider the farmer who patiently waits for the rains in the fall and in the spring. They eagerly look for the valuable harvest to ripen. You too must be patient. Take courage for the coming of the Lord is near.* If Ryan only knew how near the coming of the Lord was for him. I try to be patient as I wait for the Lord to return. I try to be courageous.

I prayed (and still pray) every day for Ryan and Shilah to be healthy and safe. We all do that as parents. But God had a different plan. I don't understand God's plan, but He loved Ryan more than I could ever love him. Someday God will tell me why, and until that day I have my faith, my trust and the heartache that threatens to destroy me but for the grace of God. His grace is sufficient! I turn to God for love and compassion and understanding because there is nothing else on this earth than can give it to me. God is the only answer. I also know this pain and loss is not about me. It was and is about God taking care of his son, Ryan, and loving him and taking him home according to His plan before he was ever formed. God is good. His heart is good. I can trust Him in the darkest night, the darkest journey and even in the valley of death. I know God's promises are true and I will see Ryan again and hold him

Tammy Stewart

for all eternity. Ryan completed his work for the Lord in sixteen years. I am still struggling to complete my work and glorify God in all He does. Grief is like an ocean wave. It pulls you to the bottom of the ocean. I have learned to be still and not fight the wave of grief. I go with it, and know it (and God) will spit me up to the top again.

God's brilliance and light and love will outshine your darkest journey! May God bless you and hold you close and cover you in His comfort and love. Eternity is coming!

Your sister in love and Christ,
Tammy Stewart

Tammy Stewart

When Only God Can Heal

Amanda Summers

*Authors note. This is a story taken from my real life. I have forgiven everyone who may have acted in a toxic way toward me and do not wish anyone to receive harassment or negative attention due to my writings. I have withheld certain names to help prevent this. I want the reader to see how I healed from these situations and not focus on the events that happened specifically. May God bless all who read this especially those in difficult circumstances.

We live in a fallen world and there are some situations that are so evil only God can bring comfort, healing, and wisdom. I have found through my experiences God must be fully trusted when you find yourself in these difficult types of situations or Satan will use the foothold created by them to further attack. I have experienced Satan doing just that in my life. I have been in some very negative situations, but most of the impactful ones seemed to follow a reoccurring theme of sexual immorality. It wasn't until I began to fully trust God and stopped trying to fix or deal with things myself that I was able to find healing and begin to move out of this cycle. Through God's healing process I have learned a lot about human nature, and have found the sliver of hope in bleak and hopeless situations. While I have had many trials throughout my life, the ones that I am sharing with you had a very big impact on me spiritually and emotionally.

Thus far there are four big trials I have undergone. They started at an age when I was not only unequipped to handle the situation, but I was also unable to recognize how bad the situation was until I looked back on it later in life. In our fallen and imperfect world, many people divorce and my parents were no exception to this trend. After they finalized their divorce, they both promptly entered into new relationships, so at the tender age of six years old I had two new step-parents. As a small child I assumed that the people my parents brought around were good and meant no harm. At six I was blissfully unaware of sex and the sexual nature of adults. In my naiveté, I didn't realize my step-father was sexually inappropriate with me until years later. While I was never raped, I was barraged with inappropriate touching and was constantly watched while I changed and bathed. The unwanted attention really bothered me. I tried to talk with my mom about it. Either she didn't believe me, or believed my step-dad. He said he didn't watch me bathe on purpose, it was because we had just one bathroom. She believed it was an innocent mistake. He had been diagnosed with mental problems, so she was sure it was just due to that. I was uncomfortable with it but tried to deny it was happening or that it was a problem.

As a child and teen, I naively thought God wouldn't let anything bad happen to a child, especially one that believed so strongly in Him. In reality, God promises us the opposite. John 16:33 promises us that "in this world you will have trouble." I thought I just had to reach eighteen, get out of my parents' house, and then I could just start my life. I didn't know all of this would have a tremendous effect on me. I told myself, *Well I was never raped, so I must not have been abused.* Then, *This shouldn't affect you because you don't want it to.* I thought if I wanted to feel a certain way, I could just will it into being regardless of the circumstances. So I ignored this first event and thought if I mentally buried it I would be healed, and I'd never have to think about it again. I never asked God for help. In retrospect I question whether it happened in order to turn me into his arms and grow me as a person and Christian. Ignoring and suppressing is how I dealt with many of my intense trials for a long time. It wasn't until the fourth and final in this series of trials that I woke up to healing God's way and not trying to heal my own way.

At eighteen I moved out and on with my life. I attended a technical college in a metro area as a computer engineering major. During this time I entered into my first serious relationship with a fellow student in my major. About six months into the relationship my lease was up. I had no girlfriends and no good options for living alone. I moved in with my boyfriend and began a physical relationship with him, which led me to become pregnant at eighteen from a broken condom he chose not to tell me about.

I was several weeks late for my period and Cinco de Mayo was approaching. He and his roommate decided to throw a party. I didn't want to drink since my period was so late and I was afraid I was pregnant. Yet he pressured me to drink and we ended up playing a drinking game. He, like most abusers, had a way of always manipulating me into doing what he wanted. The next week I took a pregnancy test which was positive. I felt so terrible for drinking that night and intensely worried that I had damaged my baby's brain. Three months later I miscarried the pregnancy. I will always feel in my heart that night of drinking lead to my eventual miscarriage of the baby.

While it was probably a good thing that I miscarried due to the abusive situation, it was not a pleasant experience to go through. I turned away from God due to the resentment I carried toward Him for putting me through this after I endured such a turbulent childhood. At that time I believed in God, but had only read the Bible once as a child. I didn't really understanding biblically why you needed to abstain from sex. I didn't fully understand the Bible and was not planted in a good church. I had been raised without any church or religion in my life. My parents said parts of the Bible were outdated rules that didn't apply to society today. They advised a physical relationship before marriage to help avoid a divorce like they experienced. It was a very bad choice.

This particular trial occurred because I did not follow God's word. If I had abstained from sex until marriage, I would not have gone through a miscarriage. I know it was not God's will for me to be unequally yoked with an abusive man. Had I known and understood God's word,

I would not have had to deal with this situation. Had I been planted in a Christian community to help me understand and study the word of God, I may have been saved from particularly painful events. Without being raised in a practicing Christian household and having been told by my step-dad not to trust churches, as they are all corrupt, I made bad choices. I also did not learn appropriate sexual boundaries during childhood.

Looking back, I wish this event had led me to seek God and study His word rather than turning me away. I strongly feel if I had followed the internal nudging God gave me in college to join a church, many challenges would have been avoided. I see this with other fallen individuals I know. Instead of turning to God for comfort, many tend to turn away or blame Him, rather than looking at ourselves to understand how we got into the situations to begin with. Not following the rules God has given us, leads to trials in our lives.

My heart was hardened and I became involved with a controlling, and emotionally and physically abusive man. I was a mess and had just lost a baby. I turned to my closest friends for advice. Two of them offered me a place to live and a way to get out of the abusive relationship. Since one was a devout Christian, I felt that I would be in a safe place, even though both were men and I'd be the only female living in the house. I foolishly thought, *If someone is of the body of Christ, they are a good person who rarely sins, and I am safe around them.*

About six months after I had moved in, I realized just how wrong I was. I'd gone to a house party without my roommates. I was nineteen and legally shouldn't have been drinking. The Bible calls on us to follow the laws of the land we are living, but I was raised in a non-religious house and was unaware of this. Besides many nineteen year olds drink, and I thought I needed to too drink in order to fit in. A few hours into the party I realized I'd had too much to drink. A couple of the men at the party wanted to have sex with me and were aggressively hitting on me. I called my Christian roommate to come pick me up so I could get home, be safe and not get raped. This seemingly smart plan turned out to be anything but. I made it home, into my own bed, and passed out. I woke up several hours later with my Christian roommate on top of me raping me. Instead of getting myself out of a bad situation I ended up in one.

It was devastating to the little remaining faith I had. I was mad at God for allowing this to happen, I went from trusting church people to hating them passionately. *All church goers were the biggest group of judgmental hypocrites in the world*, I thought. This was the beginning of spiritual darkness for me. But one of the longest spiritual deserts I experienced later led to the most spiritual and intellectual growth in my life.

During my time in the spiritual desert, I moved on with my life trying to put all of this behind me and rarely thinking about it. Several years passed and I thought I was fine and healed, since I was able to ignore it. I met my future husband and got engaged. We lived together, once engaged, on the advice of our parents and peers. Approximately a year later I got pregnant. Shortly after our son was born we were married. Our plan was for me to be a stay-at-home mom and provide him with the best start we could. We moved in with close relatives, in a metropolitan area from a small mountain resort town, in order to make a one income budget work. I had a beautiful son, a loving husband, and I loved being at home raising my child. I finally felt like I had gotten my life on track and for the first time ever, I was living life, not just surviving it. I had finally beaten my demons and could lead a normal life. Spirituality was not a part of my life at that time, and I believed I was happy. I felt religion and spirituality brought struggle to one's life.

When my child was about a year and a half, he began having night terrors and became extremely picky about the food he ate. I was extremely alarmed by the sudden changes in behavior and asked my pediatrician what could cause this. He said, "Sometimes nightmares occur because something scared them, like a tumble during that day. He was probably just developing and exploring his environment. You should not worry." My mother's intuition told me more was happening. As a first time mother I wanted to believe the pediatrician, since he had more experience than me. No matter how hard I tried to ignore the situation, the anxiety and worry persisted. I went to the emergency room twice with anxiety attacks without realizing what triggered them.

I felt something was not right with my child and I needed to figure out what it was sooner, rather than later. I kept getting a sense of God telling me to walk away from that house and never return. My child's night terrors continued and got more frequent and intense. I started to wonder if something was happening to my child when he was not in my care that was causing these terrors.

The only other person caring for my child for any significant time was a close relative we were living with. I worried it was something happening when he was with her. I started to closely watch how she interacted with him. I realized she was using corporal punishment with him, which was unacceptable to me as he was under two. Then, while attending a family function, I saw her French kiss my son. I reacted with shock and horror when no one else there reacted to this. I asked her, "What are you doing?" She replied, "Your son started it." All the family present felt this was an acceptable answer. I realized I needed to talk to my husband, and as a unit we needed to confront his family about their inappropriate behavior.

When confronted, they denied doing anything wrong. She said "If you want to continue living here, I need at least an hour a day of unsupervised time with your child." This sent up every red flag in my head, and I immediately moved me and my child out of their house. We moved in with my dad in a different part of the state until my husband could find an apartment for our family. Staying with this close relative was no longer a safe option for my son or me, since I had called them out on their completely unacceptable behavior. They now viewed me as an adversary instead of family.

Once we moved out, my son had begun talking in complete sentences and the things he said left no doubt in my mind he had been abused by them in every way possible. Soul shattering, this brought all kinds of hatred towards God bubbling to the surface. I thought, *Not only has he allowed me to be abused as a child, but he let it happen to my son too.* I had always tried my best to be a good person. *Why was this happening to me?* I wondered. *Why couldn't I escape this type of trial?* These questions and many more flowed through my mind and vexed me to no end. Instead of hating God, I decided to study His word to see if I could make any sense of why these repetitions kept happening. Why couldn't I seem to fully heal myself, no matter how hard I tried?

An amazing thing began happening when I studied God's word. My faith in Him was totally restored and God changed my heart to a heart of love toward Him. He gently showed me I wasn't just living IN a fallen world, I was living OF the fallen world. I opened up to a big realization. Trials that happened in my life were self-induced, due to the way I was living. Not just the trials I am sharing with you here, but countless others as well. God also taught me a lot about human nature and what sin nature truly means. We are all born with a sinful nature and must constantly struggle against it in order to be good. Some of us may struggle more than others, but all of us struggle.

I learned my idea that God protects those who believe in him is also untrue. Jesus promises almost the complete opposite in John 16:33 *I have told you these things, so that in me you may have peace. In this world you will have trouble. But take heart! I have overcome the world.* Reading this verse was life changing. I now understand why it is an often quoted verse. It explained why bad stuff happened to me in spite of loving God and trying to be a good person. It also told me how to find peace, something I had desperately longed and prayed for my whole life. The verse gave me hope that I could be fully, truly and completely healed. No more lying to myself and ignoring my feelings. No more trudging on, hoping I would feel better without doing anything to make it so. No more relying on time to heal the wound. I found a tool I had been missing and searching for. The perfect peace of Jesus.

I have learned two truths during my healing process. In most situations in which we want to run from God, we should run toward God. When we are angry with our circumstances and feeling most hopeless, most want to give up faith and try to go it alone. What we don't see is the spiritual warfare happening around us. Satan uses these situations to put his hooks in us, to try and lead us down the path of temptation and sin. God with all of His might and power can remove Satan's hooks and allow the healing process to truly begin in earnest.

I am often reminded of the story in Mark 9 of Jesus healing the boy possessed by an impure spirit. Only Jesus was able to heal the boy, not the disciples, despite their faith and belief. In this same way, there are many emotional situations in this fallen world in which you can only be healed through Jesus, God, and the Holy Spirit.

Secondly, through God, good will always come out of these situations. It may not seem like it at the time, and you may personally never know of all the good the situation brings, but it will bring good. Someone close to you may be watching you handle your difficulties and be inspired to learn more about faith, based on something you say or do. You may hear a testimony which later helps a fellow church member or friend, when they are going through a trial of their own.

We know John 16:33 states, *In this world you will have trouble. But take heart! I have overcome the world.* We can also find in James 1:2 that we are told to *consider it pure joy...whenever you face trials of many kinds.* The more I study the Bible, the less shocked I am I have had so many trials in my life. In fact, I consider it a privilege. Paul says, *I want you to know my dear brothers and sisters, that everything that has happened to me here has helped to spread the Good News* in Philippians 1:12. I like to think that is true for everyone and not just Paul, and all my suffering is helping to further the kingdom of God. In 2Timothy 3:12 Paul also says *everyone who wants to live a godly life in Christ Jesus will suffer persecution.* I feel this is because the fallen world persecutes the Jesus they see in you. The fallen are in the dark, and the more fallen the world and people become, the more uncomfortable they will be around Godly people. This will cause the persecution of the righteous to increase as time goes on. This leaves me feeling that I must be doing something right spiritually to have a life filled with more trials than one should have at my age. While I am still working through healing from some of these, I am at peace with having gone through them. I would never wish the emotional pain I endured on anyone, but I would wish that everyone could have the kind of close trusting and faith-filled relationship with God these struggles have brought to me. I have learned to trust God's plan, even when I don't understand it. I have also learned, even when it seems all hope is lost, God will find a way to put that window of hope into your life.

By sharing a portion of my story with you I hope that your

relationship with God is strengthened without the need to go through such difficult trials in your own life. At the end of the day, our physical bodies are fleeting and it is only our spiritual selves that are eternal. Having a relationship and trust in God ensures us an eternal existence of peace and joy. I am personally willing to walk through many trials in this temporary physical world to insure a perfect peace in the eternal spiritual world.

Love, Light, & Blessings,

Amanda Summers

CPSIA information can be obtained
at www.ICGtesting.com
Printed in the USA
FFOW02n2025090417
34298FF